Learning to Listen and Listening to Learn

To JC & JC

"Listening is an attitude of the heart, a genuine desire to be with another which both attracts and heals."

—Anais Nin

Learning to Listen and Listening to Learn

Empowering Visible Clarity

John Hattie and Lyn Sharratt

Foreword by John Malloy

Epilogue by Pak Tee Ng

A Joint Publication

FOR INFORMATION:

Corwin
A SAGE Company
2455 Teller Road
Thousand Oaks, California 91320
(800) 233-9936
www.corwin.com

SAGE Publications Ltd.
1 Oliver's Yard
55 City Road
London EC1Y 1SP
United Kingdom

SAGE Publications India Pvt. Ltd.
Unit No 323-333, Third Floor, F-Block
International Trade Tower Nehru Place
New Delhi 110 019
India

SAGE Publications Asia-Pacific Pte. Ltd.
18 Cross Street #10-10/11/12
China Square Central
Singapore 048423

Vice President and
Editorial Director: Monica Eckman
Publisher: Jessica Allan
Senior Content
Development Editor: Mia Rodriguez
Project Editor: Amy Schroller
Copy Editor: Lynne Curry
Typesetter: C&M Digitals (P) Ltd.
Cover Designer: Scott Van Atta
Marketing Manager: Olivia Bartlett

Printed in the United States of America

Library of Congress Cataloging-in-Publication Data

Names: Hattie, John, author. | Sharratt, Lyn, author.

Title: Learn to listen and listen to learn : empowering visible clarity / John Allan Hattie, Lyn Sharratt.

Description: Thousand Oaks, California : Corwin, [2025] | Includes bibliographical references and index.

Identifiers: LCCN 2024051205 | ISBN 9781071973578 (paperback) | ISBN 9781071973585 (epub) | ISBN 9781071973592 (epub) | ISBN 9781071973608 (pdf)

Subjects: LCSH: Listening—Study and teaching. | Communication in education. | Learning, Psychology of.

Classification: LCC LB1065 .H335 2025 | DDC 428.0071—dc23/eng/20241223
LC record available at https://lccn.loc.gov/2024051205

This book is printed on acid-free paper.

25 26 27 28 29 10 9 8 7 6 5 4 3 2 1

CONTENTS

FOREWORD

As educators, we often focus on the content we need to deliver, the strategies we want to implement, or the new technologies that are emerging. Yet, one of the most powerful instructional tools is often overlooked—the ability to truly listen. In *Learning to Listen and Listening to Learn: Empowering Visible Clarity*, John Hattie and Lyn Sharratt reveal how transformative listening can be for teaching, student learning, and student engagement.

John Hattie's Visible Learning research has reshaped our understanding of effective teaching by pinpointing which practices have the most significant impact on students' growth and achievement. His work underscores that learning is most powerful when it is visible—when students engage deeply and comprehend their own learning. Lyn Sharratt, with her expertise in educational leadership and classroom practice, brings these insights to life in the everyday realities of schools. Through her books *CLARITY: What Matters MOST in Learning, Teaching, and Leading* and *Putting FACES on the Data*, Lyn demonstrates how to create systems, schools, and classrooms that foster effective learning. Together, they show that learning how to really listen makes a huge difference for students.

A central message of this book is the necessity for everyone to engage in active listening and that students must be taught how to do this. The Five-Ear Listening Model outlines five essential steps: "I attend, I hear, I understand, I appraise, and I activate." This model provides educators with a framework to cultivate active listening, stimulate meaningful dialogue, and encourage critical thinking and reflection.

An important insight from the book is that educators play a pivotal role in creating the conditions for active listening and reflection in every classroom and school. Every student deserves to be heard, which requires intentional effort. When we genuinely listen to our students, understand their perspectives, and respond thoughtfully, we build a more inclusive environment where *every voice is valued.*

While the focus of this book is on classroom practices, its principles also extend to leadership practices. School leaders who prioritize listening and reflection foster collaboration, trust, and shared responsibility. By embedding these practices into school culture, leaders empower their teams, creating environments where both teachers and students can flourish.

Learning to Listen and Listening to Learn underscores that listening is not an add-on to teaching; it is fundamental to effective assessment and instruction. The strategies in this book are both practical and actionable, helping educators integrate listening and reflection into their daily routines. When students learn to listen, reflect, and think critically, they become active participants in their own learning, leading to richer educational experiences. This shift reminds educators to talk less, model more, and, most importantly, listen—as outlined here.

This book is a powerful call to action for all of us. It will resonate with educators, administrators, and policymakers who are committed to improving educational outcomes for all students and fostering student-centered learning environments. In a world where schools are navigating complex cultural and social challenges, *Learning to Listen and Listening to Learn* provides a roadmap for how listening can bridge gaps and build stronger relationships. Listening is not just about hearing words; it is about understanding and empathizing in ways that create meaningful connections.

Listening is transformational—for students, for teachers, and for leaders. It is a skill that must be taught, nurtured, and practiced at every level of our educational system. As you engage with this book, consider how you can make listening, critical thinking, dialogue, and reflection more visible in your own classroom, school, and system. Ultimately, through active listening and meaningful reflection, authentic learning occurs—and our students stand to benefit from our efforts.

John Malloy, EdD
Assistant Executive Director
The School Superintendents Association (AASA)

PREFACE

The impact of a teacher being a good listener on student learning is seismic! The impact of teaching students to become good listeners on their learning is thunderous! The impact of teachers listening to their own impact on their students' learning is monumental. Simply put, listening is the process of actively receiving, constructing meaning from, and responding to spoken or nonverbal messages (International Listening Association, 1995, p. 4). Listening is more than hearing; it requires attention, comprehension, and interpretation of the message. It includes appreciation of the emotion and intent of the message. It includes enabling the receiver to connect, empathize, and collaborate with others. There are listening skills that need to be taught and to be learned, and this book is about the power of listening.

Educators are responsible for providing all students with equitable access to high-quality, differentiated educational experiences that result in *all* their students' continuous growth and improvement. To enable this, therefore, it is imperative to acknowledge that being heard by one's teacher is important, and then to establish culturally responsive and equitable classrooms in all grade levels and subject areas is critical. Kalinec-Craig (2017, p. 2) posited that students have "the right to speak, listen, and be heard," which requires teachers to be aware of their listening behaviors. That another hears, understands, and demonstrates that they have heard and understood surely is a primary marker of respect. (This does not mean you have to agree—just heard and understood.)

Accurate listening goes a step further. It involves listening with great attention, sensitivity, and comprehension. An accurate listener hears the words being spoken and understands the underlying emotions, intentions, and nuances behind those words. Accurate listening involves being fully present in the conversation, actively

> "Listening with positive intent enables connection, mutual respect, psychological calm, and greatly enriched, joyful learning experiences."
>
> Gene Reardon, Leading Counselor, Wellbeing Focus, Melbourne, Australia

engaging with the speaker, and demonstrating empathy and understanding. Accurate listening is the foundation for building powerful relations, resolving conflicts more effectively, and gaining deeper insights into other's perspectives.

- Chapter 1 outlines the definition and understanding of listening we adopt from our collective thinking.
- Chapter 2 outlines "Clarity: The Five-Ear VISIBLE Listening Model" we have developed which underpins the discussion throughout this book.
- Chapter 3 focuses on Listening Together and discusses the power of effective, focused listening.
- Chapter 4 unpacks Listening Skills needed in school and everyday life.
- Chapter 5 focuses on Listening Practices in the classroom.
- Chapter 6 links the power of learners' voices to accurate listening behaviors. Chapter 6 asks, "Who is doing the most listening, talking, interpreting, and thinking in your class?".
- Chapter 7 helps the reader reflect on how they can measure listening.
- Chapter 8 provides a case study of how listening can enhance the school improvement work.
- Chapter 9 concludes with the pivotal role of leaders and teachers in understanding and implementing listening skills and behaviors that must be taught and modeled at every level of education.

We argue that the net outcome of a*ccurate listening* is fundamental to system and school improvement. The world thrives on accurate listening, and classrooms buzz when teachers listen to students and students listen to teachers and their peers.

PUBLISHER'S ACKNOWLEDGMENTS

Corwin gratefully acknowledges the contributions of the following reviewers:

Debra K. Las
Science Teacher
Rochester Public Schools
Rochester, MN

Deanna McClung
NBCT Science Teacher
Elkhorn Area High School
Elkhorn, WI

ABOUT THE AUTHORS

John Hattie is an award-winning education researcher and best-selling author with nearly thirty years of experience examining what works best in student learning and achievement. His research, better known as *Visible Learning*, culminates in nearly thirty years of synthesizing more than 2,400 meta-analyses comprising more than 100,000 studies involving over 300 million students. He has presented and keynoted in over 350 international conferences and received numerous recognitions for his educational contributions. His notable publications include *Visible Learning, Visible Learning for Teachers, Visible Learning and the Science of How We Learn, Visible Learning for Mathematics, Grades K-12,* and *10 Mindframes for Visible Learning.*

Lyn Sharratt is a highly sought-after expert in the field of education. A distinguished practitioner, researcher, author, and presenter, she has dedicated her career to turning cutting-edge research into practical guidance for system and school leaders. With her extensive experience and expertise, she has developed a unique roadmap for educators to utilize ongoing assessment to inform instruction and drive equity and excellence at all levels of the education system. Her work has been recognized nationally and internationally, and her insights and strategies have transformed countless classrooms, schools, districts, and even entire education systems. Her notable publications include *CLARITY: What Matters MOST in Learning, Teaching, and Leading* (Corwin, 2019) and *Putting Faces on The Data: What Great Leaders and Teachers Do!* (10th Anniversary Edition, with Michael Fullan, [Corwin, 2022]).

CHAPTER 1

LISTENING TO HEAR

There is abundant literature addressing teacher and student talk. When we delve into research on classroom dynamics, a common observation emerges. Teachers typically occupy around 90 percent of speaking time, often posing hundreds of questions that prompt brief, less than three-word responses. Interestingly, students with above-average achievement levels tend to favor teacher-centric discussions and straightforward factual inquiries, as they are the winners and find success when teachers dominate the talk and ask so many fact-related questions. One of our themes is that perhaps teachers need to budget their class time better, cutting back on their talk time and instead spending more time listening to the sounds of students' learning, listening to student questions, listening to their impact on all their students—with above average achievement, average achievement and below average achievement.

Similarly, there are abundant books, blogs, and presentations on escalating student voice. But this should not mean students talking for the sake of talking. Nuthall (2007) showed that too often students talking to each other convey wrong or false information, which can be more powerful and override what a teacher has said. As we have argued, there is a time and right place in the learning cycle for student talk, but any such talk presumes it will be heard, understood, and critically queried by other students and by the teacher (Hattie et al., 2024). Student talk, like teacher talk, presumes they are acute listeners. Yet, books in education exploring the art of listening are notably rare. Those who struggle academically yearn for an environment where teachers refrain from dominating the conversation and, instead, lend an ear focused on their thought processes. They aspire to hear fellow students and their teachers grappling with problem-solving, aiming to unravel the "magic" possessed by those who seem to excel. They want to know, "How did you do that"? Their desire is for an inclusive space where diverse voices can engage in thoughtful discourse, fostering an atmosphere where teachers and their peers understand how they are thinking. They want to hear how to enhance, support, correct, and guide themselves toward comprehension.

To be successful in education is a two-way street—both understanding and being understood are integral components. Achieving this requires honing the skill of accurate listening, creating a learning environment where the exchange of ideas is valued, and where every student feels empowered to think aloud, contributing to a collective journey of comprehension and discovery. All ideas are accepted in these spaces, and there is "'no one right way.'"

Undoubtedly, one of the highest forms of praise we can bestow upon another person is to hear their words and convey a genuine understanding of their message. This act embodies respect and an embrace of diversity but does not mean you have to agree with what is heard. Aristotle's timeless wisdom rings true: "It is the mark of an educated mind to be able to entertain a thought without accepting it."

In New Zealand culture, where we are both Pakehas, there are situations where we may not have the privilege of speaking, yet we unquestionably possess the right to listen. Listening to others is surely a fundamental mark of our respect for the speaker, the culture, and its people. By actively demonstrating our attentiveness, asking thoughtful (sometimes probing) questions, and expressing agreement or disagreement with courtesy, we contribute to a dialogue that values the richness of diverse perspectives. Winston Churchill astutely remarked, "Courage is what it takes to sit down and listen." Indeed, in the act of listening, we find not only a demonstration of courage but also a pathway to understanding, connection, and building bridges between different worlds of thought and experience.

Many theories of psychotherapy are premised on listening. Sigmund Freud, the founder of psychoanalysis, started many sessions with free association, and it was the therapist's role to listen attentively and analyze the patient's associations to uncover unconscious conflicts and thoughts. Perhaps the most famous method is Rogerian, developed by Rogers (1951, 1961, 1980). Analogous to educators, Rogers argued that therapists must embody "unconditional positive regard" for their clients. This involves actively listening, extending nonjudgmental acceptance and support, maintaining full presence and engagement, and earnestly striving to comprehend the client's perspective without imposing personal judgments or interpretations. Rogers emphasized the profound impact of authentic listening, asserting that "when someone really hears you without passing judgment on you, without taking responsibility for you, without trying to mold you, it feels damn good" (p. 69). He stressed that only after establishing such regard can therapeutic progress genuinely unfold. Lessons for educators abound here.

> An important insight from *Visible Clarity* is that educators play a pivotal role in creating the conditions for active listening and reflection in every classroom and school. Every student deserves to be heard, and that requires intentional effort. When we genuinely listen to our students, understand their perspectives, and respond thoughtfully, we build a more inclusive environment where every voice is valued.
>
> Dr. John Malloy, foreword, in *Learning to Listen and Listening to Learn,* by John Hattie and Lyn Sharratt, Corwin 2025.

One of us (JH) initially encountered Carl Rogers during graduate classes, where he viewed a video featuring Carl Rogers, Fritz Perls, and Albert Ellis conducting a counseling session with the same client (see Burry, 2008). Following this exposure, students were tasked with a more in-depth exploration of each therapist; JH continued to be impressed by Rogers' meticulous approach as both an experimentalist and psychotherapist. JH, along with a team, was instrumental in establishing a telephone counseling service based on these principles, and one of his first evaluation projects was researching the impact on this program (Hattie, 1978). The common message was that listening was core to the success of this service. Listening enabled a discussion about the presenting issue (which often was not the core issue at all) and established a caring relationship between caller and listener. Often, it was a caller hearing how others heard them and how others interpreted what they were saying that led to greater CLARITY to then attend to their issues or seek the most optimal professional care.

Rogers made a compelling assertion that initiating interactions with clients through "reflective listening" is essential. Unfortunately, this approach has been somewhat oversimplified, often reduced to the cliché of "Um, tell me more," or mere parroting of the client's words (Guenther, 2022). However, Rogers's concept of listening goes beyond this; it is nuanced, intentional, and at times challenging. It involves demonstrating to the client that the therapist is genuinely engaged, respecting their perspective (even if not necessarily agreeing), and conveying authenticity. Only by establishing this empathetic connection can the therapeutic process progress to the point of testing understandings—observing how the client reacts to life situations—and allowing space for the client to amend or reject the therapist's interpretations of their experiences. Rogers (1961) argued that there are *five categories of messages* sent between people that encompass 80 percent of all communication:

- *Evaluative* responses are most used, where the listener makes a judgement of the sender's message's relative goodness, appropriateness, effectiveness, or rightness.
- *Interpretative* indicates the listener's intent is to teach, to tell the sender what their problem means, or how the sender really feels about the problem,
- *Supportive* indicates the listener's intent is to reassure, to soothe, to reduce the sender's intensity of feeling.
- *Probing* indicates the listener's intent is to seek further information, to provoke further discussion along a certain line, or to question the sender.
- *Understanding* indicates the listener's intent is to respond only, to ask the sender whether they have correctly understood what is being said, how the sender feels about the problem and how the sender sees the problem.

Do you have a dominant mode? Do your students believe you have a dominant mode? Do your students each have a dominant mode?

Similarly, for teachers: practicing "reflective listening" doesn't imply projecting a blank screen. Through empathetic listening and clarifying meaning, educators can initiate the building of positive relationships that lead to fostering trust and understanding. Teacher listening serves as a model for students and encourages the development of empathetic listening skills, ultimately contributing to collaborative learning in the classroom. By consistently checking for understanding through reflective listening, teachers are essentially asking, "Is the information I'm providing suitable for your current position in your learning journey toward accomplishing our co-constructed Success Criteria?" This inquiry invites students to discuss their experiences, prompting them to think aloud, question, and respond. Simultaneously, it allows the teacher to demonstrate an ability to stand in each student's shoes, gaining insight into how they construct their understanding of the world (while not necessarily agreeing with the student). This dynamic interaction lays the groundwork for effective teaching and learning.

> Communication is two-way. We should seek to articulate better. More importantly, we should seek to listen better. Better articulation makes listening easier, but it is better listening on both sides that enhances mutual understanding and builds relationships.
>
> Dr. Pak Tee Ng, epilogue, in *Learning to Listen and Listening to Learn*, by John Hattie and Lyn Sharratt, Corwin 2025.

This involves much more than "reflection"—which can be as simple as looking at oneself in a mirror. We are the interpreters of the reflection and do not always see our biases or blemishes and certainly do not see ourselves as others might see us. It is a reflection more in terms of walking *through* the looking glass, like Alice in Wonderland, and listening to how others see us, hear us, and understand us. Too much teacher reflective research is "looking in the mirror" whereas more is needed to *hear* how others see us. This is where the power of listening becomes critical.

Contrary to the often inward and retrospective nature of educator "reflection," reflective listening incorporates a more evaluative approach. It involves critiquing in its true sense of determining the underlying logic, cross-checking with others' perspectives, and viewing the world from *the other side* of the mirror rather than simply gazing at one's reflection. It encourages a deeper exploration of varied viewpoints and a richer understanding of the complexity inherent in communication and interpretation.

Again, this extends beyond "reflection" where individuals recount and react or internalize what they've heard or done. In this case, reflection means the educator hears themselves as others hear them, grasps the emotional essence of their impact on others, and comprehends another person's interpretations and critiques of their words and actions. Too often, what one articulates may not precisely convey our intended meaning (our own children soon learned, "do what he means, not what he says!"). Empathetic listening becomes a potent tool, enabling the individual to recognize how to articulate their thoughts more effectively.

Throughout this book, we explore the profound impact of listening within a specific context: the classroom. For example, consider the context of Learning Intentions, the "why," and the context of feedback

Can we guide students to listen for, listen in, listen out for, listen closely, listen intently, listen with patience, listen with open minds, listen actively, listen with discerning ears, listen without judgment, listen between and beyond the lines, and listen with an ear to the ground?

relative to the Success Criteria: Do the students hear, understand and know how to action these Success Criteria? Are students truly absorbing, comprehending, and acting upon the feedback provided? Are we actively engaging with our colleagues' perspectives and sometimes dissenting opinions in staff meetings and Professional Learning sessions? Do we proactively seek and attentively listen to others' insights regarding areas for improvement, efficiency gains, and enhanced effectiveness? Moreover, do we possess a solid understanding of the fundamental skills associated with effective listening? Have we established operating norms for classrooms and meetings at all levels that elicit the conversation and feedback that are evident in effective systems as Learning Organizations?

We delve into the question of how we can gauge our students' proficiency in listening and how to improve our own listening behaviors. Equally crucial is the exploration of how we impart the skill of listening to both students and fellow educators.

The various dimensions of listening explored herein contribute to a comprehensive understanding of its significance in education and communication in society. Listening to really hear another's honest perspective has the power to resolve or prepare us to respond to the incredibly divisive national and global issues we face.

When we spoke to colleagues about our writing this book, a most common question was about the place of electronic devices such as smart phones as an impediment or distraction to listening. On the one hand, such devices can be positive in terms of access to information, convenience, customization, and communication. That is, students can listen to educational content, podcasts, audiobooks, access information and apps, adjust playback speed, reduce noise, and increase hearing acuity. On the other hand, they can be distracting, diminish the quality of listening and learning, and they can reduce face-to-face communication and listening.

There are five meta-analyses (no. studies = 144, est. # of students = 348,261) on the distracting presence of electronic devices, with an average effect size of –.24; and 31 meta-analyses (No. studies = 1,539, est. # of students = 167,413) on the positive use of devices, with an average effect size of .61. Teachers need to be smart about the optimal times to use these devices and ensure that they are not a distraction.

THE MANY DIMENSIONS OF LISTENING

It comes as no surprise that scholars argue that listening has many dimensions. S. M. Jones (2011), for example, posited that listening encompasses (a) cognitive processes, involving attending to, understanding, receiving, and interpreting messages; (b) affective processes, entailing motivation and stimulation to attend to another person's messages; and (c) behavioral processes, encompassing responses through verbal and nonverbal feedback (e.g., backchanneling, paraphrasing). Moreover, active listening employs verbal strategies (e.g., asking clarifying questions), while passive listening is nonverbal, such as providing backchanneling cues (e.g., head-nodding). Supportive listening distinguishes itself from other types of listening (e.g., casual conversation or conflict resolution, informational listening) as it demands that listeners exhibit emotional involvement. This involves attending to, interpreting, and responding to the support seeker's content and emotions—a complex and challenging task.

Chion (1994) argued there are at least three modes of listening: (1) Causal listening (the most common) is listening to sound to gather information about its cause (or source). "When we cannot see the cause of sound, sound can constitute our principal source of information about it." This mode can lead to high error rates and be deceiving. (2) Semantic listening refers to a code or a language to interpret a message like Morse code or American Sign Language. When learning to read, for example, we do not want our students to listen to the sound but listen to the sound as part of a more comprehensive process (e.g., working out the word and its meaning). (3) Reduced listening focuses on the attributes of the sound, independent of its cause and meaning. We listen to the whole sentence, pay little to no attention to the individual sounds, hear a song and not discern the instruments, and sort out sounds directed at us from surrounding noise.

Under the umbrella of reading, we recognize the Big Five core skills (Gough & Tunmer &, 1986): phonemic awareness, phonics, fluency, vocabulary, and comprehension—and want to add oral listening and comprehension as the sixth and seventh core skills. Unfortunately, the development of listening skills is often assumed to occur naturally, without explicit guidance, by osmosis and without help (Mendelsohn, 1984; Oxford, 1993/2019). When Hattie questioned researcher, educator, and notable author, Marie Clay, the creator of Reading Recovery, about the criticism that her work did not incorporate the "f-words" (phonemes, phonetic awareness), she clarified that these skills are indeed integral.

She said these are core listening skills. She also recognized the significance of teachers actively listening, saying that through listening to students learning to read and paying close attention to the strategies employed, we can gain insights into our students' literacy behaviors, track their progress, identify challenges, and discern their needs.

We conclude our initial thinking about listening with a summary presented in terms of the following "Big Ideas":

1. What is listening? Listening is a multidimensional construct that consists of complex (a) cognitive processes, such as attending to, understanding, receiving, and interpreting messages; (b) affective processes, such as being motivated and stimulated to attend to another person's messages; and (c) behavioral processes, such as responding with verbal and nonverbal feedback (e.g., backchanneling, paraphrasing) (S. M. Jones, 2011, Supportive Listening p. 85).

2. Listening is the zone in which inquiry begins to happen, when understanding initiates curiosity from which seeds of ideas begin to germinate.

3. Listening Comprehension is an active, strategic, and constructive process: *Attending - Hearing - Understanding - Appraising - Activating.*

4. Active or Passive? Listening is not a passive skill that is nonverbal; it can be and often is an active skill involving many complex processes, such as integrating information from a range of sources: phonetic, phonological, prosodic, lexical, syntactic, semantic, and pragmatic. The fact that students achieve this in "real time" as a message unfolds makes listening "complex, dynamic, and fragile" (Celce-Murcia et al., 1995).

5. The Cinderella Dilemma. While the other three language skills (reading, writing, and speaking) receive direct instructional attention, teachers often expect students to develop their listening skills by *osmosis* and without help (Mendelsohn, 1984; Oxford, 1993/2019 in Osada, 2004). Our aim is to be more explicit about the teaching and impact of listening.

We now turn our heads to a practical example of implementing "responsive listening" in the classroom by introducing our first "Deliberate Pause."

DELIBERATE PAUSE

To bring the tenets of this chapter together with a practical example, we are drawn to **listening as input and writing as output.** Stated simply, listening is the precursor to talking, thinking, and writing. As Margaret Meek says (Realization, p. 38), writing seems to be a perpetual and recurrent miracle. Writing begins with listening and can evolve to students selecting, from their portfolios, their best writing sample and publishing it to celebrate their learning. We believe this process of culling a portfolio of writing pieces to find the "best piece" to publish involves critical listening, speaking, reading and publishing, underpinned with active listening for feedback. Two examples of ways to publish students' writing follow. The first is a more hands-on and traditional methodology, perhaps better suited for younger years; the second uses digital technologies to produce and present.

EXAMPLE ONE

1. Have students write daily, as authors, following the Success Criteria (SC) in the Sidebar, that has been co-constructed with the class.
2. Post a visual Anchor Chart of the process for writing: Brainstorm, Story Map, Write, Read to a Friend, Revise, Present.
3. Discuss with the students what they deem their best writing piece is, using the Success Criteria (SC) to select their sample.

Success Criteria for Writers Who Want to Become Authors

I can

- ✓ Use strong and weak examples to improve my work
- ✓ Be clear about the purpose of and audience for my writing
- ✓ Use the steps in the writing process to finish a piece of writing
- ✓ Use Graphic Organizers to generate and organize ideas

(Continued)

(Continued)

- ✓ Listen and get ideas from my classmates
- ✓ Give and get Descriptive Feedback against the SC
- ✓ Use the Bump-It-Up Wall to discuss how I am going and what will be my next steps

4. Prepare the book itself:
   a. Sew 5–6 white "8.5×11" papers together down middle
   b. Using two identical pieces of cardboard, as covers, stick to a larger sheet of sticky vinyl covering (Mactac)
   c. Fold the sides and ends of sticky vinyl covering (Mactac) over the cardboard
   d. Stick white pages in middle
   e. Glue one white page to front and one to back of book
   f. Add a library pocket to the inside front or back cover, whichever the school librarian uses
5. Use computers to type stories, including a title page, and paste these onto each page of the new "book."
6. Add student artwork to books.
7. Present to librarian to put in school libraries to share with others after sharing with parents or carers.
8. Share their products with each other. Listen to the feedback: What did parents, teachers and students hear?

EXAMPLE TWO

Students:

1. Introduce a variety of technology tools, such as Google Apps for collaboration and construction and inspiration for mind mapping.

2. Use mind mapping software, such as https://miro.com/templates/ to first develop a story map with partner or small group—using persuasive text demands from the curriculum—on a controversial topic in society that they feel passionate about.
3. Teachers give direct feedback on this document (against the Success Criteria in Sidebar).
4. Complete the creative persuasive writing text.
5. Create a video trailer of their writing to entice an audience to read it.
6. Share their products. Listen to the feedback. What did teachers and students hear?

Success Criteria for Secondary Students Who Listen, Think, and Write Critically

I can:

- ✓ Step back, explore and analyze one's own role in an experience;
- ✓ Consider the different perspectives and responses of others involved;
- ✓ Make connections with relevant theories, supporting ideas by reference to and evidence from literature, research, and data analyses;
- ✓ Consider legal and organizational implications;
- ✓ Show awareness of social and political influences; and,
- ✓ Show what I have learned from the process and how my moving forward will be informed by experience and research.

Writing begins with listening. Both modalities open students to the pleasure of exercising their creativity and critical thinking in ways that grinding on facts, details, and information never will.

More than a way of knowing, supported by listening and talking, writing is an act of discovery (Realization, p. 39).

Listening is the ultimate mark of respect. That I not only listen but also demonstrate that I have listened, I honored your being . . . I do not have to agree, but at a minimum, I can hear your viewpoint: the heart of democracy, the core of genuineness, the essence of working with minority cultures.

At the end of each chapter, we close with a commitment to embedding the teaching of listening in all that we do in classrooms.

COMMITMENT

I commit to:

1. *Speaking less in my classes to impart facts and listening more and intently hearing my students' voices to inform my next classroom practice.*
2. *Reflecting on my "dominant mode" of listening.*
3. *Demonstrating to my students and colleagues I have heard and understood what they have said, before responding with my views.*
4. *Using mentor texts and rich literature to expose students to excellent writing models before crafting their own.*
5. *Bringing together Listening, Speaking, and Reading through authorship.*

The message of this book has hit home with "Sometimes, the best gift that we can offer another person is the gift of listening."

Dr. Pak Tee Ng, epilogue, in
Learning to Listen and Listening to Learn,
by John Hattie and Lyn Sharratt, Corwin 2025.

In the next chapter we develop our model of listening. . . .

CLARITY

The Five-Ear VISIBLE Listening Model

CHAPTER 2

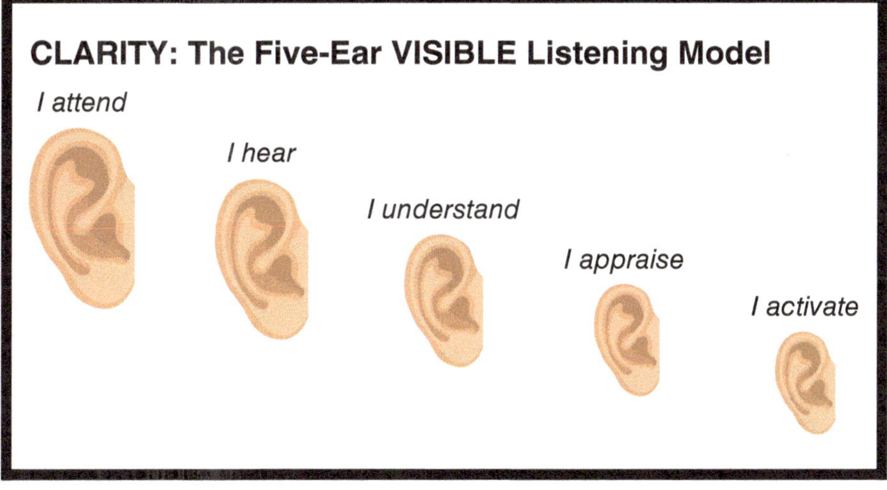

Our aim in this chapter is to identify the major dimensions of the many definitions of listening and then build our own listening model. To get ahead of the story but with the intention of helping make sense of the many parts, our model has five dimensions: I attend, I hear, I understand, I appraise, and I activate.

The earlier models had hearing as their dominant part. For example, Taylor's (1964) model was based on Hearing (the reception of speech sounds), along with Listening (e.g., attention, concentration, rate of input), and Auding (the process of hearing, recognizing, and interpreting spoken language). This latter is going to be core to our mode, as it is most relevant to teachers and students.

Then there was a flurry of models with acronyms, The MASTER model stands for Mental, Active, Sustain, Target, Eliminate, and Remember (Mills, 1974). This model emphasized that the mental decision to listen requires an active response from listeners that must be sustained by a listening target, who should work to eliminate filters and other barriers to listening, which lead to remembering. Thus, an emphasis on attention and attending. This model also identifies some of the barriers and enablers to listening and highlights the importance of remembering (and we would add forgetting or mishearing). Somewhat similar is the HURIER model—hearing, understanding, remembering, interpreting, evaluating, and responding (Bostrom & Bryant, 1980). Figure 2.1 shows

Figure 2.1 HURIER Model—Hearing, Understanding, Remembering, Interpreting, Evaluating, and Responding

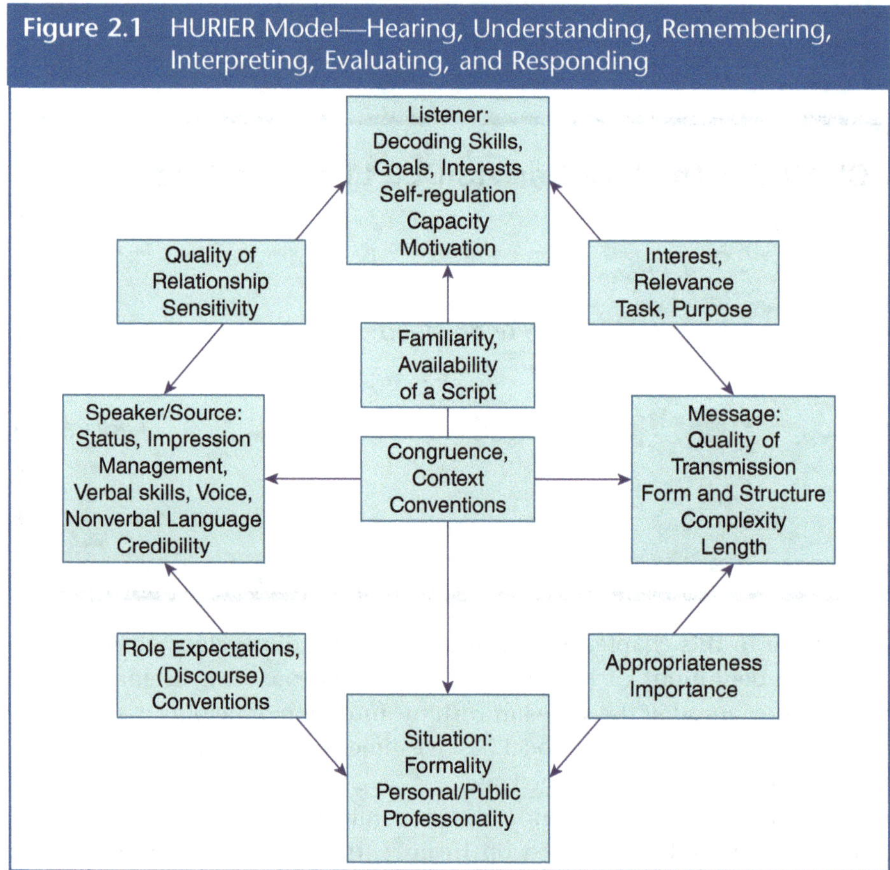

Source: Reprinted from Imhof, M. (2010). What is going on in the Mind of a Listener? The Cognitive Psychology of Listening. In *Listening and Human Communication in the 21st Century* (1st ed. pp. 97–126). chapter, Blackwell Publishing Ltd.

the various attributes of the model and highlights the many processes involved in listening.

HURIER Listening Skill Clusters

Component 1: Hearing messages
Improve concentration
Use vocalized listening technique
Prepare to listen

Component 2: Understanding messages
Recognize assumptions
Listen to entire message without interrupting
Distinguish main ideas from evidence
Perception check for accurate comprehension

Component 3: Remembering messages
Understand how memory works
Isolate and practice each memory process
Practice with difficult material

Component 4: Interpreting messages
Understand the nature of empathy
Increase sensitivity to nonverbal cues
Increase sensitivity to vocal cues
Monitor personal nonverbal behaviors

Component 5: Evaluating messages
Assess the speaker's credibility
Recognize your personal bias
Analyze logic and reasoning
Identify emotional appeals

Component 6: Responding to messages
Become familiar with response options
Recognize the impact of each response option
Increase behavioral flexibility

Source: Reprinted from Brownell, J. (2010). The Skills of Listening-Centered Communication. In *Listening and Human Communication in the 21st Century* (1st ed., pp. 141–157). chapter, Blackwell Publishing Ltd.

A more recent and greatly advanced model is by Imhof (2010). She also includes dimensions of decoding, relevance, the speaker's verbal skills, and voice. She developed a concept map of potential listening variables (Figure 2.2.) which shows the complexity of listening but also highlights the multiple considerations that become important when we listen, when we teach listening, and when we develop our teacher skills to understand the process of listening.

This led Imhoff to develop her Intention to Listen model which starts by highlighting the allocation of attention to the listening process. One of us jokes that our successful married life is because he is the world's best selective listener, and while not funny, it does point to the intentional act to also NOT listen. When we encounter people, ideas, feedback, and so forth that we may not want to hear, not want to grapple with, nor want to enact, it can be a successful strategy to intentionally not listen.

Figure 2.2 Intention to Listen Model

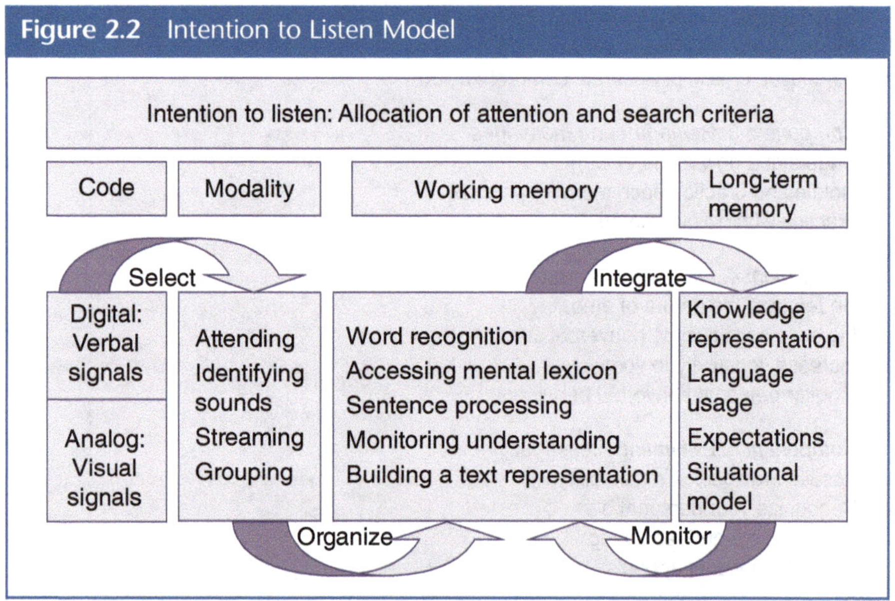

Source: Reprinted from Imhof, M. (2010). What is going on in the Mind of a Listener? The Cognitive Psychology of Listening. In *Listening and Human Communication in the 21st Century* (1st ed. pp. 97–126). chapter, Blackwell Publishing Ltd.

Imhoff noted that listeners consider "what he or she sees, hears, and knows of the speaker (What type of person is he or she? Well-meaning? An expert? A self-presenter?) and the definition of the relationship between him- or herself and the speaker (Who is this person to me? Who does this person think I am?). The message is viewed in the light of the nonverbal messages which accompany the utterance: For example, "listening to someone say, 'I am fine' with a wavering, breaking voice may elicit a different reaction than listening to someone say the same with a firm voice" (p. 111).

Imhof's (2010, 2016, 2020; Imhof & Schlag, 2016) basic notion is that listening is a constructive process—it requires the listener constructing a message. This process involves four major steps:

1. An intention to listen and this requires an investment of effort, self-regulation, and information processing,
2. Attention regulation, which involves deciding what to focus on in the messages.
3. Selected information, which is then forwarded to working memory. This requires organization, mixing with new and old information, and deciding priorities about what was said.
4. Integration of information, evaluation of meaning, and some form of responses.

Thus, listening "involves investment of intentional effort, attention, and coordination and integration of various functions." All this occurs in a context situation and presentation mode. The listening decodes messages systematically influenced by how, where, and when a message is being delivered. Imhof notes that the act of listening also communicates to the speaker various forms of reciprocity – do they care about what I am saying, are they just waiting to espouse their views, or do they intend to engage in a dialogue, monologue, dismissal, or harangue?

Imhof (personal communication) noted that listening serves a variety of purposes in the classroom. Good listening is essential both for building trust and relationships between students and teachers, for community building, and for learning. Listening situations in class include students listening to teacher-talk but also students listening to students, to media, to familiar voices, and complete strangers. Listening skills need to be highly adaptive in terms of speakers, language, purposes, knowledge, and so on.

Note also the importance of working memory, which we know from cognitive load theory can be very limiting. There can be many distractions to occupy students' minds and there can be so much going on in a classroom that a teacher may not "hear" what is happening. Nuthall (2007) showed that a teacher does not see or hear about 80 percent of what happens in a classroom. This is why, oftentimes, we need others to help us interpret what we experience and why we need technology and apps that give us other ways to "hear" what is occurring. Using collective efficacy, we also need others to help build the confidence that, together as educators, enables us to hear our impact, stand in the shoes of all our students to understand their experiences of learning, and build high trust, so that our students feel comfortable revealing their thoughts and feeling. They want to be heard, understood, and improved.

Students in schools listen more than talk; or at least some work hard to look like they are listening but indeed are not. It is worth considering Perls's (1969) observation: Verbal communication is usually a lie. The real communication is beyond the words. So don't listen to the words, just listen to what the voice tells you, what the movements tell you, wat the posture tells you, what the image tells you.

Moreover, classrooms can be noisy places, which is not necessarily bad; it can indicate the busy chatter of thinking aloud, playing with ideas, critiquing and improving together. However, we can also be distracted by noise; we can be daydreaming, listening to our tummies growling for food, thinking about how to keep warm or cool, or simply misunderstanding what is said to us and trying to make sense of what we think is gibberish.

As humans, students and teachers have biases that can interfere with, exaggerate, or distort the intention of the messages we are hearing. There are many biases (see Hattie & Hamilton, 2018), such as confirmation bias (we hear what we agree with), receiver bias (we don't listen so well to people we have low trust in or who are threatening), and opinion bias (we distort or minimize views we do not agree with and hear loudly those we do). We can be apprehensive such as not being convinced you have heard what was said correctly, worry that it is "over your head," know we are not very good at the topic, and avoid improvement information. And these can lead to "receiver apprehensions"—the fear that you might be unable to understand the message or process the information correctly or be able to adapt your thinking to include the new information coherently, or just fear of new information (Bodie & Fitch-Hauser, 2010). Preiss and Wheeless (1989), in a meta-analysis, found receiver apprehension to be negatively related to listening effectiveness ($r = -.17$), information processing effectiveness ($r = .34$), and information processing complexity ($r = .34$), and highly related to information processing anxiety ($r = .43$). They noted the vacuity of claims that the listener "just needs to relax" and instead advocated for interventions that focused upon improving information processing and listening.

Another recent model is by Thompson et al. (2010). They developed their model based on four premises: preparing to listen, applying listening processes, assessing listening effectiveness, and establishing new goals for future listening events. These were underpinned by learning attitudes, knowledge, and behaviours. It is worth considering their four developmental levels for these four premises—as this could assist in evaluating your own listening skills as well as the skills of your students (Figure 2.3).

English et al. (2023) noted that it is not only *that* a teacher listens, but rather *how* a teacher listens, and what they are listening *to* and *for* is consequential for student learning. They built a model of pedagogical listening that includes five types of listening: *empathic, supportive, educative, self-reflective, and generative.*

- Empathic listening involves listening openly to the learner's unique understanding, feelings, and perspectives regarding a concept or situation. It requires the teacher to set aside their own judgments, perspectives, and feelings to fully hear the student as a person, and it allows students to feel genuinely heard, fostering a sense of appreciation, self-esteem, and belonging.
- Supportive listening occurs when teachers listen with the intention of helping learners listen to one another, encouraging them to consider and learn from perspectives different from their own. It involves being responsive to where each student is in their thinking and helping to create connections between students' ideas.
- Educative listening occurs when teachers listen attentively to the diverse struggles students face with new ideas or interactions and seek ways to help transform these struggles into "productive struggles." It involves asking learners how they are making sense of a concept, what questions they have, or what they find confusing or challenging.
- Self-reflective listening involves listening to students' unexpected or challenging responses in a way that prompts the teacher to reflect on and potentially alter their own thinking, values, beliefs, and practices to better support student learning.
- Generative listening occurs when teachers listen for opportunities within students' dialogue to generate new ideas and directions, leading to the emergence of previously unforeseen understandings, educational opportunities, norms, and goals.

Figure 2.3 Developmental Levels

	Level 1 **Self-assesses strengths and weaknesses, identifying the attitudes, knowledge, and behaviors that helped or hindered her listening process**	**Level 2** **Shows understanding of listening as a dynamic, mindful process and identifies strategies to increase listening effectiveness**	**Level 3** **Applies the Integrative Listening Model and uses listening strategies appropriate to specific academic settings**	**Level 4** **Applies effective listening attitudes, knowledge, and behaviors consistently in personal, academic, and professional settings**
PREPARES TO LISTEN	Listens to a given stimulus as directed	Addresses the physical, mental, and emotional factors that influence the listening process	Determines goal(s), analyzes context, and addresses listening filters	Considers carefully listening goals, context, and filters and anticipates adjustments that may be required by a situation
APPLIES THE LISTENING PROCESS	Receives, comprehends, and responds appropriately to at least some part of a message	Receives, comprehends, interprets, and responds appropriately to the essence of messages	Receives, comprehends, interprets, evaluates, and responds to both verbal and nonverbal components of messages	Adapts the integrative listening process, as necessary, to attend to multiple layers of a message
ASSESSES EFFECTIVENESS OF LISTENING PERFORMANCE	Identifies some strengths and weaknesses regarding attitudes, knowledge, and behavior in a listening performance	Identifies and analyzes strengths and weaknesses regarding attitudes, knowledge, and behaviors in listening performances	Analyzes and judges specific strengths and weaknesses regarding attitudes, knowledge, and behaviors in academic listening	Shows refined analysis and judgment of own listening ability as an integral aspect of lifelong learning
ESTABLISHES NEW GOALS	Determines area(s) to develop based on a discrete listening performance	Reflects on self-assessment to determine patterns in listening performances and sets goals for ongoing development	Reflects on self-assessment to refine listening performances in academic disciplines	Reflects on self-assessment to continue growth as a listener in all settings

Source: Reprinted from Thompson, K., Leintz, P., Nevers, B. & Witkowski, S. (2010). The Integrative Listening Model: An Approach to Teaching and Learning Listening. In *Listening and Human Communication in the 21st Century* (1st ed. pp. 266–286). chapter, Blackwell Publishing Ltd.

Working with nine US and Scottish elementary teachers' interacting with students as they struggled with the ideas in the lesson, English et al. noted that "What is most striking is the ways teachers used pedagogical listening to provide "students with opportunities to explore their 'learner's rights'—the rights 'to be confused,' 'to claim mistakes,' 'to speak, listen and be heard,' 'to write, do and represent only what makes sense' (Kalinec-Craig, 2017, p. 1)—in ways they otherwise would not have had" (p. 19). These students adopted a "listening stance: that involved being "prepared to listen to, respond responsibly to, and *be with*, all learners as their thinking and struggle emerges" (p. 20).

CLARITY: THE FIVE-EAR VISIBLE LISTENING MODEL

Standing on the shoulders of others or (more appropriately, given the theme of this book) building wisdom through listening to other voices, we reviewed the many models and the attributes of the models and developed a five-step model. The model is more a pathway as they are linked, have an order, and all are critical: I attend, I hear, I understand, I appraise, and I activate. These highlight the importance for educators to be aware of the culture and context of the following: (1) attending (e.g., high trust, safety to not know and make errors (fail fast), welcome to express thoughts and feelings); (2) the skills of hearing, which are then reviewed; (3) ensuring compatibility of understanding (or not); (4) appraisals and interpretations that are made about the message and messenger; and, (5) activating, the actions that are based on the previous four steps.

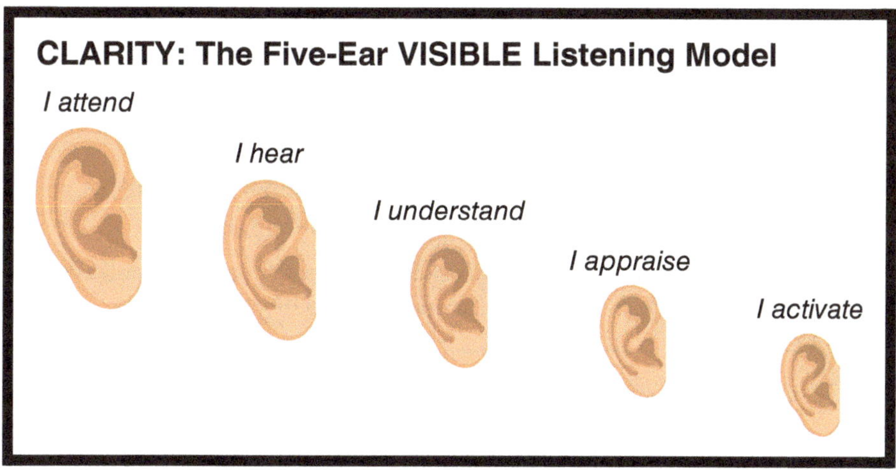

This five-step model emphasizes the importance of both cognitive and emotional aspects of listening, as well as the role of reflection and continuous improvement in developing effective listening skills.

I attend: Preparation and Mindset:

- Self-awareness: Understanding one's own biases, emotions, and communication style
- Adaptability: Being flexible in communication style and approach based on the context and the speaker's needs
- Open-to-learn stance: Being open and willing to learn from others
- Cultural competence: Recognizing and respecting cultural differences in communication styles and norms

I hear: Engagement and Interaction:

- Active engagement: Fully participating in the conversation with attentiveness and interest
- Devoting short-term working memory: Ensuring what is said is activated in short-term memory to thus increase the probability of being processed and interpreted
- Nonverbal communication: Using body language, facial expressions, and gestures to show understanding and empathy
- Concentration: Focusing on the speaker's message without succumbing to distractions or interruptions
- Time management: Managing time effectively to allow for thorough listening and meaningful responses
- Avoiding judgment: Suspending personal judgments or biases to understand the speaker's perspective fully
- Patience and tolerance: Remaining patient and tolerant, even in challenging or frustrating conversations

I understand: Listening Techniques:

- Critical listening: Analyzing and evaluating the speaker's message for accuracy, logic, and coherence
- Informational listening: Listening to gain new information or knowledge from the speaker
- Asking clarifying questions: Seeking clarification or additional information to ensure understanding
- Probative questioning: Asking probing questions to delve deeper into the speaker's thoughts, personal or organization biases or motivations

I appraise:

- Making value judgments: I evaluate, assess, or judge the value, quality, or significance of what I hear
- Empathetic listening: Understanding and sharing the speaker's feelings, thoughts, and perspectives
- Appreciative listening: Showing appreciation and respect for the speaker's perspective or accomplishments

I activate: Action and Feedback:

- Feedback skills: Providing constructive feedback to the speaker that reflects understanding and empathy
- Assessment for and as learning: Reflecting on the listening experience to identify areas for improvement and growth
- Accountable Talk and Accountable Listening: Taking responsibility for one's contributions to the conversation and holding oneself and others accountable for factual, reliable, and valid communication

The first step from "hearing" to "listening" is not as simplistic as it might seem. It involves moving from an automatic response to a controlled way of processing what is being heard. The importance and hard work of learning to attend, how to engage, and how to understand cannot be overstated, particularly given the many distractions in classrooms, the overwhelming amount of teacher talk, and the energy needed to use the cognitive resources of working out what is background and what is important. Again, learning a variety of techniques in these steps becomes even more salient for the student than to appraise what is heard. We like the notion of "appraise" since it includes a valuing component, with students sometimes valuing the critical and important notions while, at other times, valuing the peripheral and unimportant notions. As educators, we listen (we attend-engage-understand) to their appraisals and plan our feedback carefully. We realize their appraisals are the essence of their takeaways and that they will use these appraisals to take action—to form patterns between ideas, using these new ideas and patterns in assignments and tasks, which then become the basis and filters for future attending, hearing, and listening.

Learning each listening step well is critical to future learning.

DELIBERATE PAUSE . . .

Read the following quote and using a Four Square (see graphic), list or discuss with others what is (1) noteworthy, (2) a question, (3) unique, and (4) coincides with your thinking.

"Listening is a vital skill in education. Typically, students spend a large proportion (up to 70 percent) of their school day "listening"—to teachers, their peers, instructional technology, and even to their own speech as they pay attention to how they sound to themselves. Listening is essential for academic achievement, social interaction, and personal growth. However, listening is one of the least taught skills in schools (Wills, 2020). The development of effective listening skills requires explicit instruction, practice, and modeling. The five practices embedded in the five-ear listening model provides clear direction for developing deeper levels of listening and therefore learning as students attend, hear, seek to understand, appraise, and activate. As the Dalai Lama reminds us "When you talk, you are only repeating what you already know. But if you listen, you may learn something new."

Source: In Conversation with Dr. Janelle Wills, 2024, Author, Researcher, Practitioner

Noteworthy	***A question***
Unique	***Coincides with your thinking***

COMMITMENT

I commit to:

1. *Contemplating where I am on the 5-Ear Listening Continuum and determining my "next best* listening moves."
2. *Auditing how much time I spend talking as opposed to listening during my teaching.*
3. *Changing one habit in order to hear the nuances between and beyond what students are saying.*

LISTENING TOGETHER

CHAPTER 3

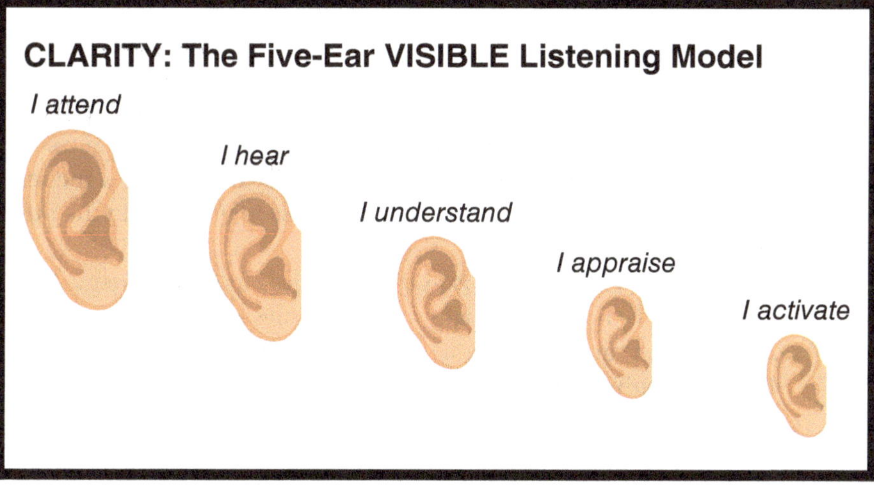

In classrooms, teachers dominate talk, and students are "required" to listen (although they too rarely listen but "surface attend" or pretend to listen, at best). While we saw in Chapter 1 that higher performing students may do well with teachers dominating the speaking platform, others do not.

> "Wisdom is the reward you get for a lifetime of listening when you'd have preferred to talk."
>
> —-Doug Larsen

THINKING ABOUT TALKING AND LISTENING

The German philosopher Martin Buber argued that too often, communication is seen as me talking and you listening with little attention to the relationships between the speaker and listener. The listener is there to hear me—I rarely check for understanding and know the other is being polite and waiting for a gap so they can talk (and I am then supposed to listen). He called this an *I-It* relationship.

Buber argued that a more powerful form of communication is the *I-Thou*. In this form, we, as teachers (the speaker), are more self-reflective of our impact on the other(s); we care about how they are understanding us; we check for understanding we listen to responses, reactions, and the other's viewpoints; and we acknowledge the nonverbal messages (e.g., eye contact, nods, and voice tone). Buber (1965) claimed "listening and learning are more powerful when there is a willingness to be open to moments where both individuals include the other in their own experience and listen for responses (I hear)." This occurs when the dialogue is more of the I-Thou relation: Each person becomes aware of the other, aware that they are different, and each accepts the uniqueness of the others and how they may be interpreting what I am saying (I appraise). Central to dialogue is the notion of empathy, which involves the temporary "suspension" of one's own concreteness to understand the other (Buber, 1925).

Most classroom dialogue is in the I-It form, but it needs to evolve to become more I-Thou. This chapter reviews issues relating to the interaction of speaker and listening, of listening together, and ensuring high levels of empathy between teacher and students, students and teachers, and students with students.

CLASSROOM DIALOGUE AND LISTENING

When we speak in the classroom or as leaders in the school or system, we often do so with the intent that the other person cares about what we say, interprets what we say, or acts upon what we say. When we speak, however, we too often do so to speechify—just to tell others with little attention to check for understanding. Indeed, classroom observation research shows teachers give many "speeches," and they dominate the talk in the classroom. Clinton and Dawson (2018) found 89 percent of the talking time is by teachers. Students are relegated to listeners, attendees, or daydreamers. Many students learn to withdraw or avoid listening and just come back into focus when asked to undertake some activity (often showing confusion as they were not engaging with the teacher talk). Teachers talk *at* rather than *with* their students (Galton, 1995); and most of this talk is at a low cognitive level (Hargreaves & Galton, 2002) absent of higher-order questions, answers, and thinking. This encourages "cruising"—pretending to listen, turning off, and daydreaming. Yes, a small percentage listen and respond, reinforcing teachers to continue talking.

Yes, teachers do have methods for checking and this is commonly referred to as the IRE model of interaction (Nystrand et al., 2003; Smith et al., 2004). The teacher **Initiates** a question, the student **Responds** (the typical response is less than three words), and the teacher **Evaluates**. For over 80 percent of the teacher questions asked, the teachers already know the answer (Shomoossi, 2004); most of the questions are closed with low cognitive demands on students (see Asay & Orgill, 2010; Erdogan & Campbell, 2008; Nystrand et al., 2003), and the most common form of interaction is still the IRE cycle. When teachers evaluate, they praise correct responses and correct errors (although < 3 percent of the time they use errors as opportunities to clarify). Lefstein and Snell (2011) estimated that within one year, the typical teacher poses over sixty thousand questions and follows up student responses with over thirty thousand evaluations. So, throughout school life, students are asked over half a million questions with very little checking by the teacher as to why the student submitted the wrong answer. I-It continues to dominate the class. The I-Thou classroom checks whether the student is attending, hearing, understanding, appraising, and activating.

In the earlier work on classroom discussion, Flanders (1965) observed the "two-thirds" principle: That for about two-thirds of most class lessons, somebody is talking; that about two-thirds of this talking is done by the teacher; and that two-thirds of teacher talk is talking "at" students. Class discussion is rare (less than fifteen seconds a day in English and about thirty seconds in Social Studies classes); more than 60 percent had no discussion at all, and another 15 percent had no more than two minutes per day (Nystrand et al., 1998). These seminal findings were mirrored in the MET study of three thousand classes, where 60 percent of the classes did not have a single classroom discussion over three months (Kane et al., 2013). Students are demanded to "listen." Tragically, classes are dominated by I-It—hence our passion in writing this book together.

One of us (LS) was in a secondary classroom recently and quickly noticed that the students were paying rapt attention to the speaker. "Why were they so attentive?" I needed to know. I soon realized that "the speaker" was the teacher of this Grade 9 class who was engaged in Modelled Reading (better known as "Think Aloud" in the Gradual Release/Acceptance of Responsibility model (Vygotsky, 1978). She was moving as she read; she was modulating her voice from character to character, and she was screaming at one point—so much so, that the students were on the edges of their seats, and I was glued to mine. Students seemed to flinch at the desperate cries of the hero and heroine and then relax as the scene ended with the dropping of the gun. What made this group of students understand the rapid dénouement in this play? Why could they react authentically to the terror felt by these characters? I realized it was all about the investment in teaching and learning, in listening and hearing, that this teacher had perfected.

Interestingly, the whole class had perfectly demonstrated the five stages of our listening model. These students could follow the playwright's ingenuity (I attend) and express genuine concern for the characters (I hear and understand), demonstrating these emotions in their own reactions (I appraise). Following the reading, the teacher had them express their reactions in writing (I activate). This teacher had made a strong, personal connection to her students' appreciation of the rich literature by "living in" her teaching and "living out" her own learning.

Classrooms with high levels of clarity in attending, hearing, understanding, appraising and "acting on" listening opportunities capture the listening skills of students in ways that witness an increase in students' comprehension, leading to higher-order thinking.

"THE WHY" OF SO MUCH TEACHER TALK

The reason for so much teacher questioning relates to the mind frames about teaching and learning held by many teachers—that is, their role is to impart knowledge and information about a subject, and student learning is the acquisition of this information through processes of repetition, memorization, and recall. Hence, there is a need for much questioning to check that students have heard and can recall the information they impart. When students haven't grasp the concept being taught, we often hear teachers reteaching the concept in the same way, only louder and longer!

We ask you to think differently about teacher talk—the aim of teacher talk is for students to attend, hear, understand, appraise, and activate. Students need time and acknowledgement that they can check what they heard, can understand and know how to activate what is heard, and be given the opportunity and safety to ask clarifying questions. Like the proverbial tree falling in the forest, teachers talk in so many classes but if students do not attend, hear, understand, apprise, and activate, were there any sounds at all?

However, it is not as simple as teachers talking less and students talking more. Goodwin et al. (2020) analyzed the classroom talk of about twenty thousand fourth and fifth grades and their 745 language arts teachers. They noted four dominant modes: teacher explaining, teacher questioning, teacher encouraging student talk, and teacher summarizing learning. The one factor that did *not* relate to student learning was increasing the proportion of student talk. This was because too much student talk was about their perceptions of quantity not quality and did not involve critical thinking. Students too often emulate teachers: Talk in facts, seek a response, and evaluate the response. Student talk is particularly a concern when it involves summarizing learning because such summaries too often are about the teacher's (not students') beliefs about the *what* (not the *why*) of the learning, and too much is tied to knowledge acquisition rather than critical thinking.

> "The fact that students differ may be **inconvenient, but it is inescapable**. Adapting to that diversity is the inevitable price of productivity, high standards, and fairness to kids."
>
> —Theodore Sizer

Classroom discussions (not IRE types) can be a beneficial two-way mechanism to differentiate instruction, including teachers to hear feedback and for students to engage in a dialogue of learning (I attend), hearing (I hear—understand), alternative interpretations (I appraise), and become more engaged (I activate) in the learning process (Alexander, 2020; Mercer et al., 2019). Classroom dialogue is thus dynamic, relational, and mediated by experiences with others.

How then can teachers create dialogic classrooms:

- Collaborative Reasoning (Anderson et al., 1998) encourages students to use reasoned discourse to choose among alternative perspectives on an issue, invites students to adopt a position on the issue, and generates reasons that support their position.

- Questioning the Author (Beck et al., 2020) asks students to examine the author's position as an "expert," to read against the text, and to presume that difficulties they encounter when reading challenging texts are not necessarily attributable to their inadequacies.
- Book Club (Raphael et al., 2001) comprises four elements: reading, writing, engaging with this reading, and writing in small-group discussion (book clubs), and sharing with the class.
- Computer-based Knowledge Mobilization Forum developed by Scardamalia and Bereiter (2006) invites students to collectively investigate problems by adding individual notes, graphs, build-ons, and rise-above-it notes.
- The Scratch Community Bulletin Board (Roque et al., 2016) allows students to receive feedback from others. The Web of Inquiry system supports students in generating theories, constructing hypotheses, and conducting and analyzing their investigations.
- Co-constructing sentence stems that promote Accountable Talk and Listening and model how to build on the ideas of others: "I understand what Robbie is saying and add that. . . ."

> "Listen with curiosity. Speak with honesty. Act with integrity. The greatest problem with communication is we don't listen to understand. We listen to reply."
>
> — Roy T. Bennett

Specjal (2022) noted that what matters is what teachers and students do before, during, and after discussions. The *before* or priming stage requires at least a basic understanding of the text before participating in a discussion (I attend). *During* discussions, teachers should aim to promote meaningful interactions by challenging student responses, scaffolding, and demonstrating norms of discussion (I hear—understand). Teachers can also (*after*) gradually release responsibility to the students so they can co-construct and "interthink" understandings of the text (I appraise). Such discussion requires students to externalize their cognitive processes (think aloud) (I activate), and teachers can "listen" to how students process the text to help inform them of their 'next best teaching moves'.

An important note here: you can't get higher-order answers from low-level questions! Teachers and leaders must consider modeling higher-order verbs in developing Learning Intentions, Success Criteria and Questions, for example. The following graphic from St. Edwards University (FACES, 2022, Appendix F, p. 311) demonstrates the verbs teachers and students must plan to use in daily conversations and performance tasks.

Figure 3.1 Questions and Tasks Predict Performance

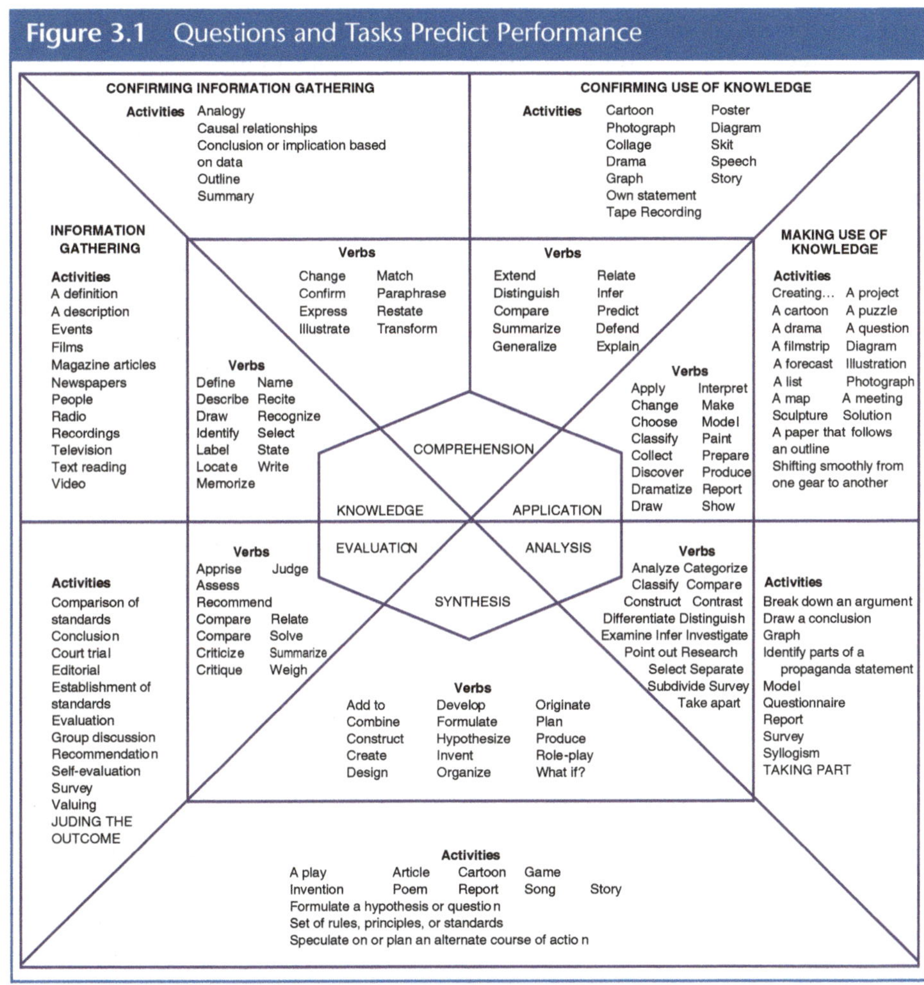

Source: © 2004 St. Edward's University Center for Teaching Excellence.

STUDENT QUESTIONING

We love to ask questions, seek answers, and contemplate next questions. Sometimes when we do not get answers, this raises interest, and we seek multiple sources. For example, "Who invented the names for the continents" and "Why is tiny Europe a continent and India just part of a continent"? MS Google, ChatGPT, and encyclopaedias fail to answer these questions, so they remain great mysteries, an intrigue, and a conundrum—which is why it is fascinating to ponder meaningful questions. We're happy to engage in many years of "wait-time" for an answer (and probably a touch disappointed when this happens as the thrill is in seeking enlightenment). The search for an answer can be as much fun as finding answers. Socrates presumed we already knew, and thus his method was aimed at eliciting the answers from the students, inviting them to self-discovery, to seek multiple sources, and promote connections (I activate).

Asking questions is easy, *but the hard part is asking the right question at the right time, for the right purpose, and with the right level of complexity.* Indeed, with the new AI apps, developing competence in asking probative [probing] questions becomes a necessary skill. These AI apps will answer every question no matter how poorly worded, often giving the right answer to the wrong question. As JH wrote in the preface to an impactful book on questioning (Chiles, 2023), "As educators we spend so much time on devising the right question when our aim maybe more to elicit the right response—maybe inviting students to contemplate, use learning strategies to come to the right answer, work with others to prioritize the optimal answer, or to elicit wrong answers so as to better understand how they are thinking. What an unusual profession where the purpose of questioning is not simply to get the right answer!" (Hattie, 2023, p. i).

> AI can be a useful tool for teachers to learn to ask powerful, specific questions rather than fearing that AI is something that will only enable students to avoid the hard work of writing something new. . . .

MORE ABOUT PROBATIVE QUESTIONING

"Probative questioning" typically refers to a form of questioning aimed at eliciting relevant and helpful information in determining the truth or accuracy of a matter. ChatGPT generated some benefits of 'probative questioning':

1. Is an Effective Tool for Investigation: Many investigators and legal professionals praise probative questioning as an effective tool for uncovering crucial details and evidence. By focusing on questions that directly relate to the issue, probative questioning helps cut through extraneous information and get to the heart of the matter.

2. Enhances Fact-Finding Processes: Probative questioning is often lauded for enhancing the fact-finding process. By asking precise and targeted questions, individuals can gather pertinent information more efficiently, leading to a clearer understanding of the situation under investigation.
3. Promotes Objectivity and Fairness: When conducted properly, probative questioning promotes objectivity and fairness in various contexts, such as legal proceedings and investigative interviews. By avoiding leading questions or biases, interrogators can ensure that the information obtained is reliable and unbiased.
4. Encourages Critical Thinking: Engaging in probative questioning requires individuals to think critically about the information they seek and the responses they receive. This process encourages both questioners and respondents to consider the relevance and reliability of the information, leading to more informed decision-making.
5. Minimizes Misunderstandings and Miscommunications: Probative questioning aims to clarify misunderstandings and minimize miscommunications by asking clear and direct questions. By fostering effective communication, this approach helps prevent confusion and ensures that all parties involved clearly understand the issues at hand.
6. Facilitates Resolution of Disputes: In dispute resolution processes, probative questioning can be instrumental in uncovering facts and resolving conflicts. By guiding parties through a structured questioning process, mediators and arbitrators can help identify common ground and facilitate agreements.
7. Can Be Intimidating or Overly Aggressive: Some critics argue that probative questioning, if not conducted carefully, can be intimidating or overly aggressive. This can lead to defensive responses from witnesses or reluctance to provide information, ultimately hindering the investigative process.
8. Requires Skill and Training: Effective probative questioning requires skill and training to ensure that questions are relevant, unbiased, and properly framed. Without adequate training, individuals may inadvertently ask leading questions or overlook important details, undermining the integrity of the questioning process.

While "probative questioning" is widely recognized for its ability to uncover relevant information and enhance decision-making processes, it must be conducted with care and precision to ensure fairness, objectivity, and impact.

DIALOGICAL TEACHING

Dialogical teaching is a model that engages students in dialogical and dialectical discussions and guides them to develop thinking that is clear, precise, specific, relevant, consistent, logical, and rational. Such discussions involve extended exchanges between different points of view or frames of reference. In these discussions, individuals consider the strengths and weaknesses of opposing points of view and pit two or more opposing points of view in competition with each other. Venn diagrams support students thinking about opposing views.

Figure 3.2 Venn Diagrams Support Dialogue and Thinking

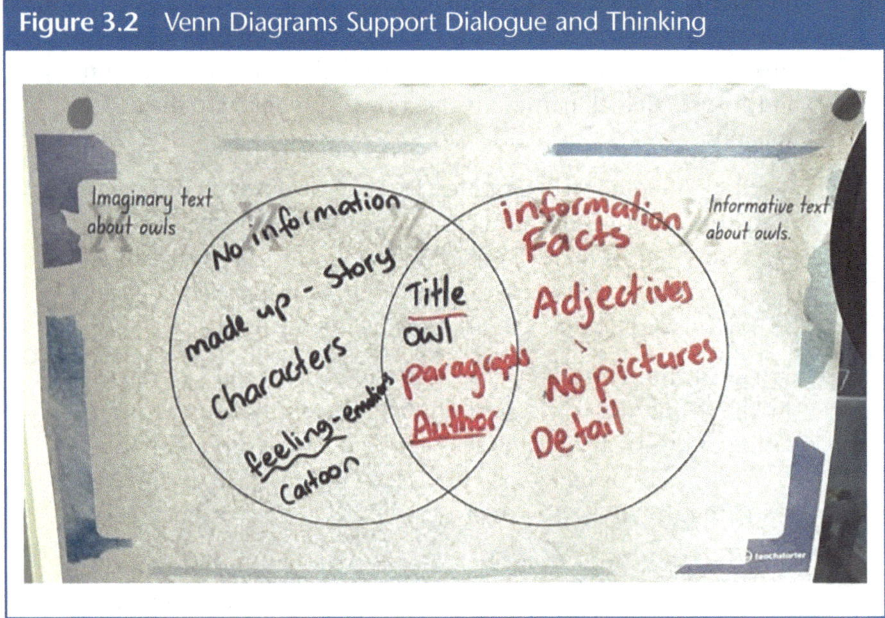

Source: Photo by Dr. Lyn Sharratt

Students learn to support their views, raise objections, counter those objections, and raise new objections. They learn to seek knowledge, data, or the truth about knowledge beyond the uncritical thinker's understanding.

As our consistent assessment approach, we must rethink and embrace in-class listening, thinking, and creating.

The model often includes Socratic questioning strategies that raise basic issues, probe beneath the surface of contents, and that help students to develop sensitivity to clarity, accuracy, and relevance (Paul & Elder, 2007). Socratic questioning techniques help teachers to keep the discussion focused (I attend), intellectually responsible (I hear—understand), and stimulating (I appraise). Teachers probe for intellectually responsible answers (I activate) by periodically summarizing what has and has not been dealt with.

There have been nine meta-analyses (no. studies = 270) on the influence of teacher questioning on achievement with an overall **effect size of .51**, and seven meta-analyses (no. studies = 360) of student self-questioning with an overall **effect size of .53**. Imagine the **effect size** if we moved beyond the factual, the accurate, the IRE schedule. We noted above the high number of teacher questions a day and now note that there are about two questions per day per class from students about what they do not comprehend—not counting procedural questions (what page are we on? etc.). So often *students want* to ask, "Why is this so?" whereas *we ask,* "What is so?". Teachers ask more for recall, low level questions, whereas students want to understand and appraise (critical thinking questions).

It should be no surprise that so many student questions in class mimic our use of the IRE schedule, expecting less than a three-word answer by the teacher, and thus missing a richness and a skill development opportunity for students to engage in by asking more impactful questions. As Chiles (2023) notes, "The greatest attribute of questioning is that it stimulates thinking in the classroom," and questioning is "the single most influential teaching act" because they [the questions] empower students to attend, hear, understand, appraise, and activate critical thinking. Surely our aim is not to develop quiz kids full of facts, providers of three-word or less responses to others factual questions, or to ask questions to which they already know the answer.

Chiles (2023) also noted the various purposes of questions. Questions can inform the teacher of their impact, lead to different directions in the lesson, and invite joint teacher-student investigation of answers. He investigates the ways to build a questioning culture, increasing student questions, and explains beautifully how to use questions so students can:

- ✓ check for understanding;
- ✓ move from lower to higher order questions (and back again);
- ✓ question to assess progress against the co-constructed success criteria; and,
- ✓ question each other to build student collective efficacy about their learning (I activate).

> Video yourself teaching before and after reading this book. Note the switch you have made from IRE dominance to sharing the questioning with students and note how students become ***more engaged*** in the learning when they—as attentive listeners—take on the role of proficient questioners (appraisers) and activate their own learning—the ultimate!

While teacher questions are ever present, this should not mean we underestimate the importance of questions—particularly students' questioning each other. Further, questions from students can provide powerful feedback to teachers about their impact and help students engage in the wonder, the depth, and curiosity, aiding them in achieving deeper *clarity* in their learning.

Not all questions are the same. Boaler and Brodie (2004), for example, examined mathematics classes in terms of nine categories of questions:

- ✓ gathering questions requiring an immediate answer (more than 95 percent of the questions asked by teachers were of this first form);
- ✓ questions inserting terminology;
- ✓ questions exploring points;
- ✓ probing questions getting students to explain their thinking;
- ✓ questions generating discussion;

- ✓ questions linking and relating among ideas;
- ✓ questions extending thinking;
- ✓ orienting questions that help students to focus on key ideas'; and
- ✓ questions establishing context.

Nystrand et al. (1998) have argued that the two most powerful questions were "uptake" questions whereby teachers validate particular student ideas by incorporating their responses into subsequent questions and "authentic" questions—questions asked to obtain valued information or questions without "prespecified" answers not simply to see what students know and don't know.

> "Authentic questions, like uptake, also contribute to coherence. By asking authentic questions, teachers elicit students' ideas, opinions, and feelings, making students' prior knowledge and values available as a context for processing new information. (thus they) . . . contribute to the coherence of instruction by enlarging the network of available meanings in the class" (Nystrand et al., 1998. p. 7).

In any subject area, at any grade level, teachers can use the answers to authentic questions to form co-constructed Success Criteria which become waypoints for future self-checking in a learning unit.

Nystrand et al. (2003) also noted that the rates of student questions were lower in low-track classes (along with more off-task behavior and less completing of assignments). In these classes, discourse tends toward monologue and fewer uptake or authentic student questions—a vicious cycle. Note: In providing discussion concerning equity and excellence across the teaching/student learning spectrum, the two-level questioning and answering issue of high track versus low track capability is not being ignored or dismissed here.

Similarly, Chiles (2023) outlined two attributes of good questions from teachers or students:

- A good question reflects a genuine desire to find a deep feeling for wanting to know more than we already know.
- A good question helps us to think—that is, a question that is transcendent, one that helps us move beyond the immediate data or experience.

CREATING A SAFE CULTURE OF QUESTIONING

Sharratt (2023) argued that when we engage in "intentional listening" we:

- listen to recharge, reenergize, and renew to experience the elegance of success and progress.
- are willing to "fail fast," willing to try multiple approaches to elicit responses when first, second or third attempts are not working.
- drop or modify that "not so" approach.
- know where to go for help for better teaching ideas and are not too proud to ask.

As intentional listeners, educators listen to be culturally responsive (I attend) and learn to recruit energetic, passionate people with a similar deep sense of urgency for the vision of *all* students' learning (I hear and understand). Intentional listeners in the classroom and the staffroom engage in a delicate balance between offering the speaker validation (I appraise) and challenging them to improve (I activate) (see also Kluger & Itzchakov, 2022).

As listeners, we make decisions when others are speaking, including detecting or predicting the consequences of interacting with that speaker, whether to compete, cooperate or ignore, and whether it is safe to engage in dialogue or react to the speaker. Thus, intentional listeners need to be cognizant of their own listening to others and to the reactions and visibly demonstrated thinking/listening behaviors of their listeners. Where there is a power relationship (as in most teacher-student interactions) and there isn't this culture of safety to be wrong ('Fail Fast'), it can be tough to say, "I do not understand," and to engage in dialogue. When that positive, "open-to learning stance" doesn't exist, as Rogers (1951) noted, we reverse to habitual routines—look like you are listening, agree, and move on or out—and try to learn from that experience to listen and respond more fully in the next similar instance (I activate).

> Surely, as Kluger and Itzchakov (2022, p. 138) claim, "participation in the togetherness experience leaves both conversation partners with *clarity*, novel plans, new knowledge, heightened well-being, and strengthened attachment to each other."

STRATEGIES TO ENCOURAGE ENGAGEMENT AND PARTICIPATION

Alongside convincing you of the critical importance of scaffolding to create higher order questions comes a discussion of some of the most powerful processes for integrating them into every lesson.

1. **Response cards.** One of the downsides of whole class questioning is the low participation of many students in answering the questions. Randolph (2007) found that response cards were powerful in increasing participation (by 50 percent) and were preferred (82 percent) to hand raising. Response cards are cards, signs, or items that all students in the class simultaneously hold up to display their responses to questions or problems. Students using response cards, on average, performed d = 1.08 higher on quizzes and d = 0.38 higher on tests than students in the hand-raising condition.
2. **Teach Thin and Thick questions and answers.** Listening and responding in a higher-order way can be taught by teachers' modeling and visually representing the quest for robust thinking in every classroom as demonstrated in Figure 3.3

Figure 3.3 Thin and Thick Questions and Answers

(Continued)

(Continued)

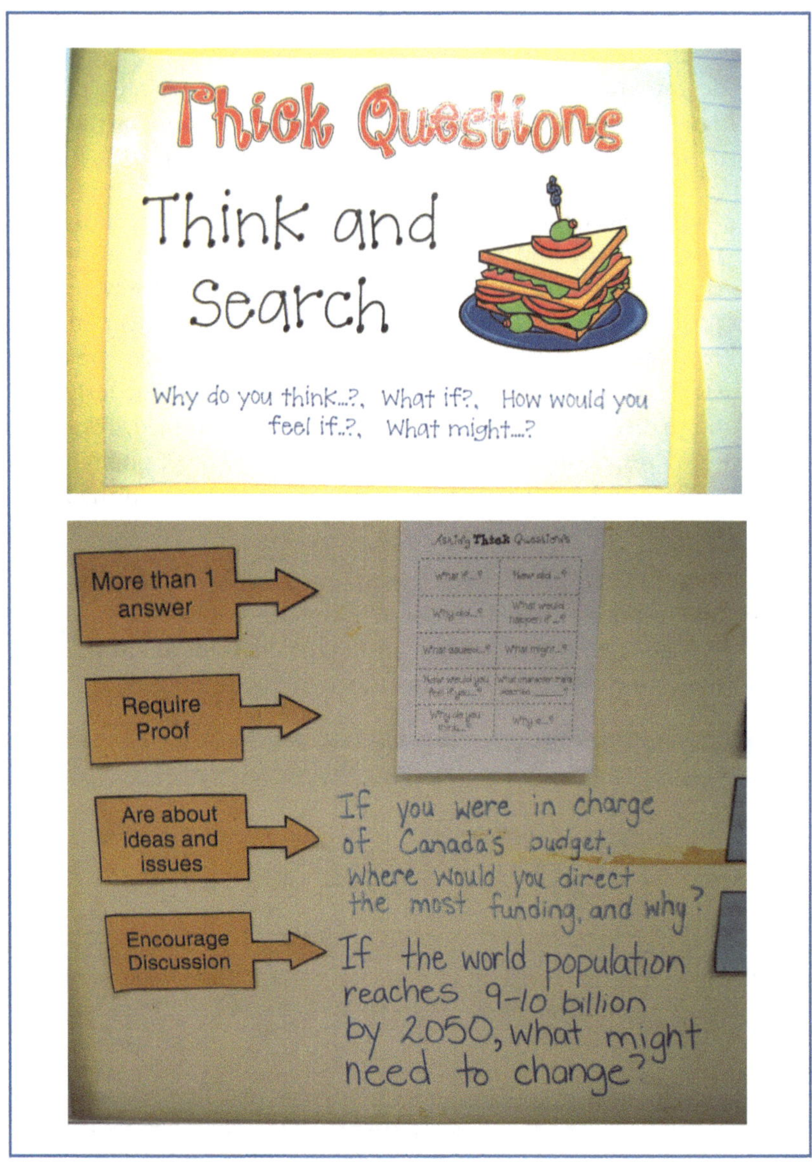

Source: Photos by Dr. Lyn Sharratt

3. **Randomly ask students for viewpoints, answers, and what they are pondering.** Asking "what do you now not understand" rather than "do you understand" (when so many are conditioned to give the expected answer, "yes").

4. **Welcoming the wrong answer.** No child comes to the class to learn that which they already know, although what they learn can be based on what they already know. Some learn that it is dangerous to not know, particularly when peers confirm they are "not smart" and teachers pass them by when asking for answers to questions. Errors become embarrassments rather than opportunities to learn. In some subject areas and discussions, questions that set up a directional content response enable teachers to query students who they feel should respond more often but to do the querying in a relatively non-threatening way (Fail Safe). A wrong or unexpected answer can become a jumping-off point for a teacher's response or that of another student who should be asked "to build on this please . . .". This welcoming not only builds that sense of trust in the class, the trust by the particular student in the teacher, but it clearly models the type of response a teacher should want in a fully participating classroom.

5. **Developing Empathy** speaks to developing student collective efficacy (**Effect Size: 1.57**), the I and We skills, listening to others, standing in the shoes of others (empathy), synchronizing verbal and nonverbal messages (see Hattie et al., 2021).

MAKING CARING CONNECTIONS TO FACILITATE ENGAGEMENT IN LISTENING

In schools with visual, tangible Data Walls located in <u>private</u> places accessible only to leaders and teachers, Sharratt (2019) recommends that teachers sign their initials on the students' Data Tags if they have made a "Caring Connection" to that FACE (see Figure 3.4).

Figure 3.4

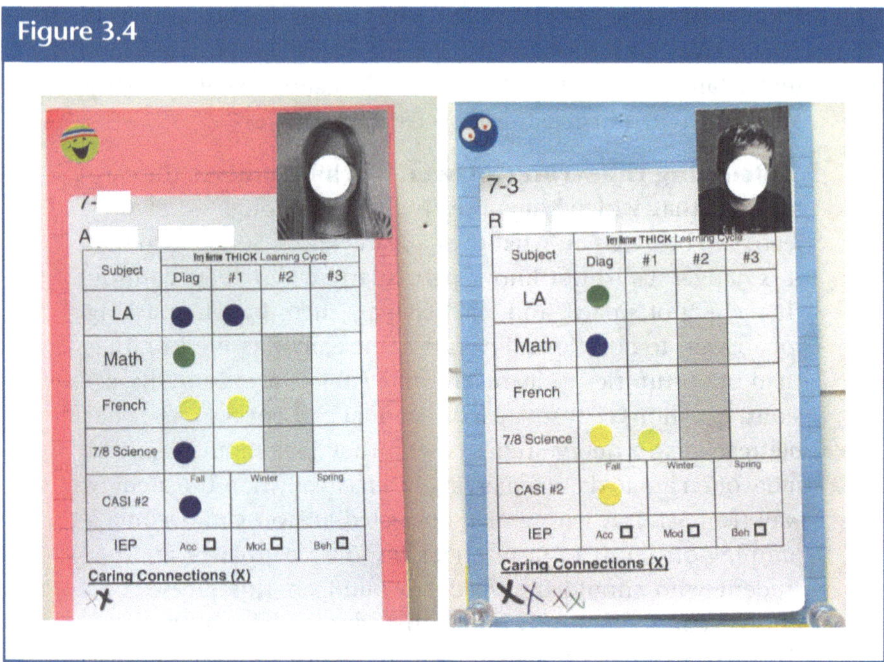

Source: Reprinted from Sharratt and Fullan, 2022.

Caring Connections are defined by staff before this activity begins, including descriptors of what attending, hearing, understanding, appraising, and activating look and sound like when having an empathetic conversation with that student. This strategy offers particular promise when a student is not or appears to be unable to respond to questioning in a class but can in another. The cue seen by one teacher may often be invisible to or unheard by another. The advantage of this strategy is that it brings well-being and learning together. At a glance on the Data Wall, you can see which students have "caring connections" to one or more teachers and which students have none. Then it's time to act, as "omission is commission."

DELIBERATE PAUSE . . .

Attentive listening must be taught—it does not develop on its own! In parallel, substantive questioning does not develop on its own. Chiles's (2023) writing demonstrates the latter. When students hear thin, closed-ended questions, they respond in kind with thin answers that aren't very growth-promoting for themselves or their classmates. When asked thick, open-ended questions, causing Higher-Order Thinking (HOT) their answers become thick answers. Thin begets thin; thick begets thick. As examples:

Thin Question: "What color is Sally's dress? Thin Answer: "purple."

Thick Question: "How do we ensure that the planet is protected from climate change?"

Thick Answer: "There are multiple solutions to consider; here are three of many possibilities: Stop burning coal to reduce greenhouse gas; reduce, recycle, and reuse waste to reduce the use of fossil fuels in finding new resources; ensure that examples of climate impact already underway such as rising ocean levels are moderated, for example, by protecting seacoasts and populations who are affected by current changes.

Thick answers are worth exploring by peers—they only happen by listening, that is, attending, hearing, understanding, appraising, and activating thinking and exploring—and are a must in every classroom.

At every year level, we need to strive to assist students to co-construct the Success Criteria to listen and speak using "Thick Thinking" and to develop critical thinking questions that then elicit thick answers as in figure 3.5.

Activity: Develop anchor charts with students and staff of examples of thin questions and answers and thick questions and answers to develop classroom and staff room learning walls.

Our critical message is that listening skills must be scaffolded and taught in every K–12 classroom (and beyond!) and that teachers and leaders must be trained to model good listening practices using effective questioning methods. Once taught, they must be commended for continuing to use those good questioning practices.

In the next chapter, we will consider the Listening Skills needed to become contributing global citizens.

Figure 3.5 Anchor Charts of Success Criteria for Thick Questions and Thick Answers

Source: Photo by Lyn Sharratt.

COMMITMENT

I commit to:

1. *Attending to and intently hearing* students' *voices to inform my practice.*
2. *Understanding the research that points to the power of higher-order questioning to get higher-order "thick" answers.*
3. *Monitoring the open-ended questions I ask and the wait-time I allow so critical thinkers can develop in my classes.*

LISTENING SKILLS

CHAPTER 4

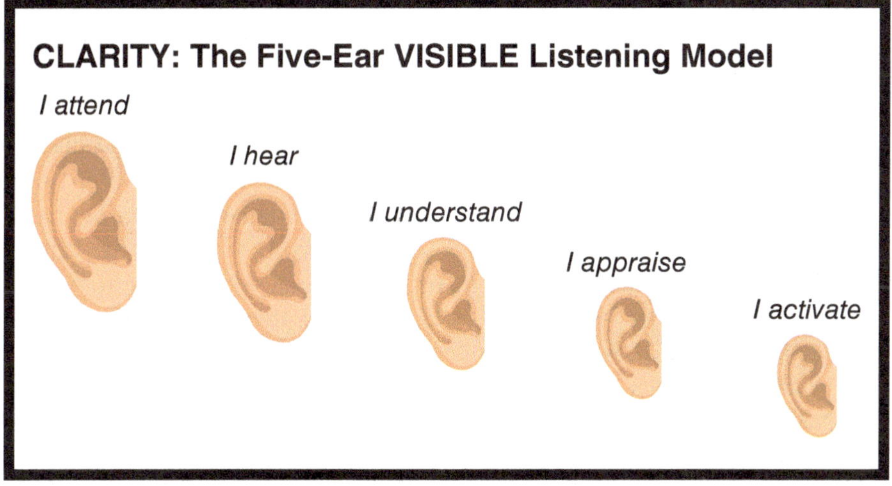

In this chapter we discuss the learn-able listening *skills* within the communication dialogue skill set of "Active Listening" as described by Nelson-Jones (2014). They wrote that Active Listening means fully attuning oneself to the feelings and views of the speaker, demonstrating unbiased acceptance and validation of their experience.

Extending beyond simply hearing words, Active Listening requires the listener to engage with the speaker (I attend), to demonstrate genuine interest, comprehension and empathy (I hear and understand)—the response part of dialogue without actually speaking (I appraise and activate). Active Listeners are always processing information heard through five self-assessment questions, displayed in Figure 4.1.

Figure 4.1 5 Questions for Listeners

- ✓ What am I hearing?
- ✓ What connections am I making to self, others, and the world?
- ✓ How do I ask for clarification?
- ✓ What feedback can I contribute?
- ✓ Where can I learn more?

It is "deep work" for many of us who are not always attentive listeners, who may not have time to listen to "all that stuff." It goes to the heart of good teaching and good leading at all levels. As educators, we must strive to know how well we are being understood in order to become the communicators we must become. So, let us take you into the deep work in which we consider the soft skills teachers and students need in order to be attentive listeners. At the end of the chapter we will take a Deliberate Pause, using a reflective activity to help you make sense of the deep work.

To begin, we go back to the key concept—bias in listening, hearing, and understanding—and to the supporting notion of the Ladder of Inference (Senge, 1990). As listeners, our experiences, our expectations, and our sense that others should think and express ideas similar to those we espouse, believe, and understand, get in the way of—in fact often block—actually hearing what is being said. In every Learning Organization (Sharratt, 1996), the halo effect of our own biases blocks deep listening. We must recognize the difference between the usual process of listening and hearing what we want to hear, and Attentive Listening in which we use learned skills (attend, hear, understand, appraise, activate) to reduce the impact of our biases on what is being said.

1. TEACHERS LISTEN!

Listening in the classroom begins with teachers' ability to "hear" and "understand" what is being said or produced by students, and teachers' desire actually to know the learners in front of them. Teachers need many listening skills as an integral part of their personal art and science of teaching. For example, some of the many skills that teachers need to integrate into their teaching repertoire follow:

- ✓ **Understanding Student Needs**

  By actively listening to students, teachers can better understand their individual learning needs, challenges, and interests. This understanding allows for more personalized and targeted instruction. Students all begin at different places. The differences in the families' capacities to satisfy basic student needs can be a hidden detractor to classroom learning. Those without the necessary food, dress, or sleep needs must be supported in some way. The impact of differences in access to technology and of English language resources between students will be very visible and will reduce the number of learning options immediately available to students. Differences in cultural acceptance, where for example, asking questions of parents (which many foster as curiosity) may be deemed to be an intolerable break down of parental authority or an unacceptable intrusion. Dealing with student learning disabilities may be a "non-starter" in some families. These and others are foundational starting points which once recognized must not be permitted to enter the biases of teachers, other students, and school leaders.

- ✓ **Building Relationships**

  Attentive Listening fosters positive teacher-student relationships. When students feel heard and feel the opportunity to express their opinions is protected and that they are understood, they are more likely to engage in the learning process, trust their teachers, and contribute to the class conversations. Informal day-to-day interaction and attentive listening by the teacher will build ongoing positive relationships. Data Wall notations from other teachers and Caring Connections, when available, are invaluable sources of background data for relationship building. Others have found that descriptive, student-driven assessments such as "Tell Them from Me" (The Learning Bar) used in Canada and Australia provide valuable input, some of which would otherwise not be known and the lack of which could hamper learning of many students in many classrooms.

✓ **Effective Communication**

Teachers, who actively listen as they prepare for instruction, communicate more intentionally with others than those who do not, widening the gap even more as they continuously "check for understanding." They clarify instructions, respond appropriately to questions, engage others in classroom discussions, protect all opinions, and provide constructive descriptive feedback. Teachers who embrace Active Listening skills (described above) (Nelson-Jones., 2014) know the importance of using and visualizing deconstructed Learning Intentions and co-constructed Success Criteria to build common language in the class thereby focusing all students' listening, speaking, and thinking skills (Sharratt, 2019, p. 124). These teachers also become leaders of choice, showing Knowledge-ability (Sharratt & Fullan, 2022) and very authentic concern.

✓ **Promoting Inclusivity**

The elements of Attentive Listening include recognizing and eliminating personal bias and creating an inclusive learning environment where all students feel valued and respected. That in turn encourages diverse perspectives and experiences to be acknowledged and integrated into classroom dialogue.

✓ **Addressing Misconceptions**

In checking for understanding of student work, whether written or verbal, teachers promptly "listen" intently to identify and address misconceptions or misunderstandings of the learning. By attentively listening to students' questions, comments and discussions, or descriptive feedback, any misconstrued facts or tasks/processes can be addressed quickly, ensuring that the intended task is appropriately and completely understood and the learning underway is accurate and meaningful. Importantly too, the willingness to listen and exhibit change also models powerful leadership and interpersonal behavior from which students can learn.

✓ **Encouraging Critical Thinking**

Attentive Listening promotes critical thinking skills by encouraging students to express their thoughts, to formulate and ask meaningful (thick) questions, and to engage in thoughtful discussions beyond the facts already heard and learned. Listening for the cues to unpack the capacity of students to think critically is imperative in providing relevant feedback. Anchor charts and Bump-It-Up Walls (Sharratt, 2019), classroom spaces where expectations are visual and progressive, in learning spaces, in all subject areas, at all grade levels, enhance students' ability to analyze information, think critically, and evaluate concepts on their own before taking their own next steps to improvement.

✓ **Creating a Supportive Classroom Environment**

A classroom where Attentive Listening is prioritized tends to be more supportive and collaborative. Students are more likely to participate, share ideas, and collaborate with their peers when it is a safe environment in which to listen and speak up. Classroom operating norms, especially those that address the need to ensure every voice is heard and that every discussion includes clarification and elaboration rather than attacking statements or opinions, will create that necessary environment or culture of supportive learning. By using classroom walls to provide "co-constructed knowledge" as the "Third Teacher" (Sharratt, 2019, Chapter 1) not only is there support for learning but the learning becomes more collaborative, layered or nuanced and student-centered. When teachers and students co-construct classroom walls as learning walls, students are enabled to "own" their own learning and become less dependent on the teacher for all the answers. (See Figure 4.2.)

✓ **Classroom Management**

Teachers who employ Attentive Listening skills can better understand classroom dynamics. By modelling purposeful listening (I attend, I hear, I understand, I appraise, I activate) with their students, they will positively impact classroom management and, therefore, will decrease disruptive behavior and increase learning potential. A critical part of classroom management is reflecting on the flow of learning. Effective listening requires allocating sufficient time for interacting, thinking and reflecting. Time constraints must be considered; however, prioritizing quality interactions over quantity (covering the given material) is necessary, which engages students in listening more attentively.

Figure 4.2 Sample of Co-constructed "Third Teacher" as Learning Support

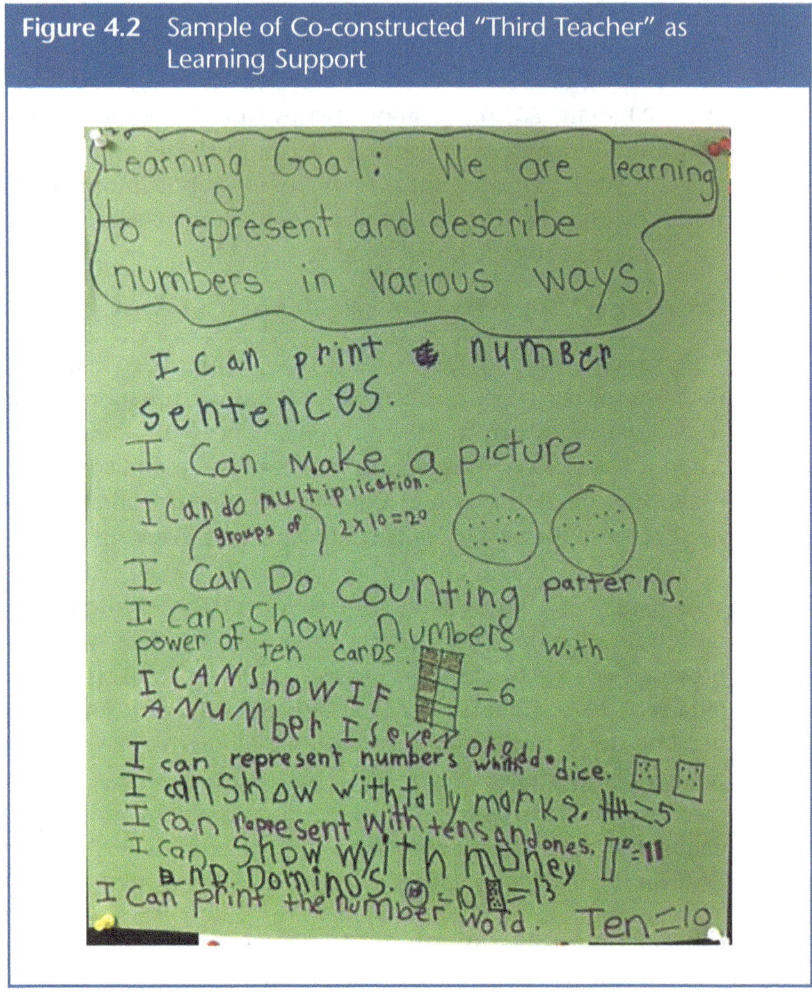

Source: Photo by Dr. Lyn Sharratt, Manitoba, Canada

✓ **Continuous Improvement**

Teachers can continuously improve their instructional practice by gathering feedback through Attentive Listening from observing the reactions of students to their instructional strategies (did that work? or did it not work, and why?). As discussed in Sharratt and Fullan (2022) and Sharratt (2019), teachers who employ the co-teaching cycle, Figure 4.3, can also build strength upon strength to continuously improve their practice focused on intentionally teaching listening skills in the classroom.

Figure 4.3 The Co-Teaching Cycle

Step 1: Co-Plan

- Find protected time with a trusted colleague or KO to plan, teach with video, debrief, and reflect
- Discuss what you each want to improve about your practice to give each other Descriptive Feedback during the process (your Collaborative Inquiry focus)
- Begin with the curriculum expectations, then plan the assessment to deconstruct the Learning Intentions, co-construct the Success Criteria, and provide a cognitively demanding performance task for students to be able to demonstrate their learning (Chapters 4 and 5)
- Plan the before, during, and after the lesson (Chapter 4), thinking about flow, timing, and pace
- Plan to use research-proven, high-impact instructional strategies differentiated based on student need (Chapter 5)

Step 2: Co-Teach

- Set up a digital recording device, like the swivel camera if possible, to follow the voice and images of the moving teachers
- Work side-by-side in a classroom
- Co-facilitate classroom Accountable Talk, hearing every student's voice
- Observe during teaching, "Who is doing the most talking and the most thinking in the classroom?"
- Monitor students' self-assessment by asking them, "What are you learning? Why? How are you doing? How do you know? How can you improve? Where do you go for help when stuck?" (See Chapters 2 and 9.)
- Change pace and flow if necessary
- Give ongoing Descriptive Feedback to students against the Success Criteria
- Check for students' understanding and learning against the Success Criteria

THE CO-TEACHING CYCLE

Step 3: Co-Debrief

- Examine the video clip to look/listen for: more students' voices than teacher voice; higher-order questions and responses; creative critical thinking; students' use of the Success Criteria; students self-assessing and self-correcting
- Discuss teaching practices and prompts used
- Assess if the taught, learned, and assessed curriculum-based Learning Intentions were aligned using student work samples as evidence
- Give each other Descriptive Feedback about the Collaborative Inquiry question that each wanted to improve about his or her practice, looking closely at the video clip as a personal data source
- Use work samples to assess students' understanding and learning growth against the co-constructed Success Criteria. Ask, "Were they the correct Learning Intention and Success Criteria?"
- Decide what needs revision

Step 4: Co-Reflect

- Discuss the co-teaching process: What worked? What didn't work? What would we do differently next time?
- Engage with partner in an open, honest dialogue about improving practice
- Identify and understand what changes in practice and beliefs need revision for you each to become consciously and competently skilled
- Plan next steps for students' and teachers' learning in this cycle of inquiry

Source: Adapted from Sharratt and Harild (2015).

Understanding what resonates with students and what actions in their own classroom work allow for ongoing adjustments and enhancements to teaching approaches. This is critical to understanding one's professional persona and capacity to improve.

2. STUDENTS LISTEN!

Similarly, it is crucial for students to develop a collection of effective listening skills. Becoming proficient in these skills plays a key role in their academic success, personal relationship-building, and optional choices regarding potential career or life pathways. The following are some essential listening skills that students must learn and practice, which teachers must teach and ensure are used by each student.

✓ **Attentive Listening**

As it is for teachers, Attentive Listening essentially means students learning to self-regulate to focus on remembering the task at hand. This involves paying attention to what other students or teachers are saying, simultaneously determining what that message means to them within their own current base of knowledge and emotion, and how they feel the information might fit into the broader classroom, community, or world context today and tomorrow.

A key element for students is learning **how to use** the Operating Norms (Figure 4.4), co-constructed with teachers, to respect each other and maintain those values of listening in order to build on the ideas of others. Adopting and learning how to use the models of reaction and interaction that positively impact conversation and feedback are crucial. Practicing making eye contact, nodding to indicate comprehension (note this does not mean agreement), responding to fellow students and the teacher appropriately within the context of the Operating Norms, and avoiding classroom distractions are other critical factors in students becoming active, attentive listeners. The operating norms in Figure 4.4 were co-constructed by voices across the school and have been displayed as an expectation.

Figure 4.4 Operating Norms Establish a Culture of Listening and Learning

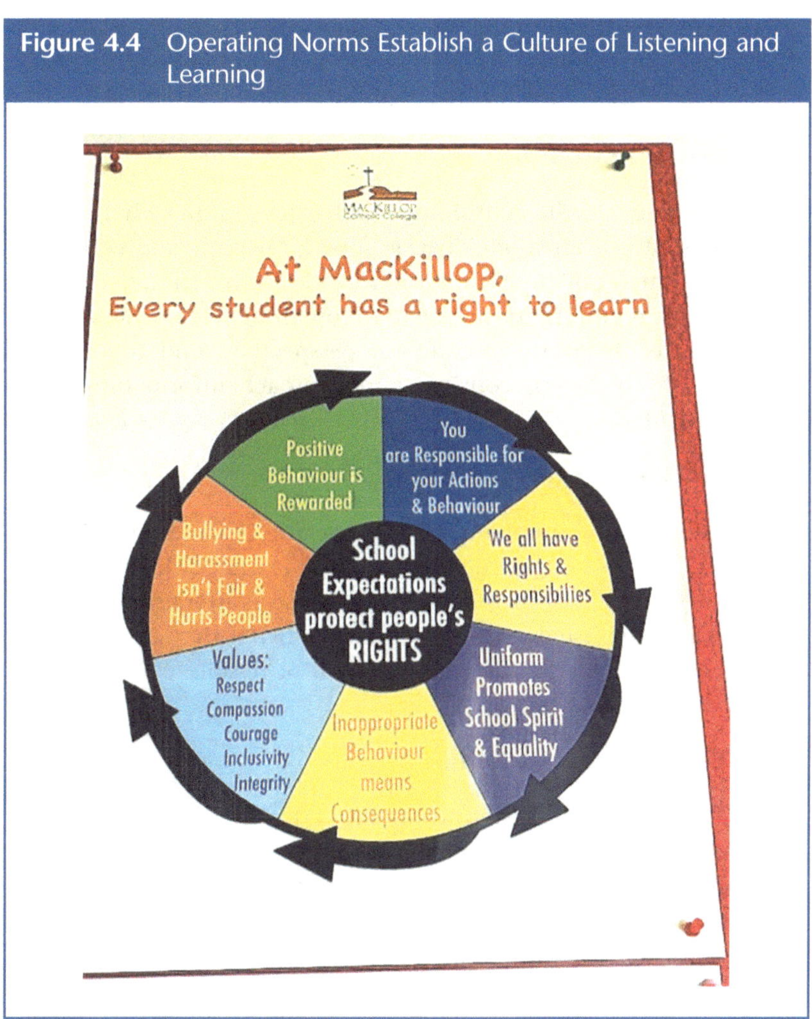

Source: Images by Dr. Lyn Sharratt

✓ **Selective Listening**

As important as it is at times to hear everything being said, sometimes it is as important to concentrate on listening for specific information within a verbal response or presentation while filtering out the irrelevant details. Who decides what are relevant details and which are irrelevant? That is at the heart of selective listening. It is also the heart of preparing to present reports on topics or responses to questions or in-class debates in a logical, coherently argued manner. Only what matters, matters.

- ✓ **Critical Listening**

The steps in critical listening involve questioning what is being presented against one's background knowledge and evaluating the impact of the information on decision-making. This also means retaining the ability to follow these steps while remaining keenly aware of different perspectives and biases from which they each consider and approach information being presented (I attend, I hear, I understand, I appraise, I activate).

- ✓ **Clarifying Questioning**

Elaborating on thoughts by asking clarifying questions demonstrates active engagement and a genuine interest in what others have to say. Learning to ask these questions after listening is crucial to the listeners' understanding of what they thought they heard and to the speaker to re-form or re-state what has been said for greater clarity.

- ✓ **Empathetic Listening**

The key part of the definition is that the listener moves beyond the facts being presented and engages with the emotional tone of the presenter—expressing empathy. Understanding the emotional undercurrent while not being swept up in it gives the listening student a deeper sense of the argument, proposition, or idea being delivered by peers or teacher. The key part of listening with empathy is to not become judgmental, rush into supporting the notion because of the depth of emotion being heard or observed or close the door on the proposition due to the same depth of emotion. The important part of this listening skill is to hear the emotion of the presenter, to understand how that emotion impacts the presentation—to try to understand how the facts or emotions have swept the presenter to think this way—and yet be able to "cut away" from that substantially while thinking critically and making a decision or judgement about what is being heard or seen (I activate).

✓ **Informational Listening**

More a process of listening and recording data than listening and sorting emotion, the sorting of critical facts becomes a mechanism for recording what noteworthy information is being heard. Students learn how to capture the main points of what is being said using various note-taking styles, but students have to be taught how to do this using several different strategies and then assess which is the best for themselves as individual learners. We, as educators, know our strategies in differing situations (our own shorthand, the way we organize dot points, the way we rewrite notes as we study); all of these strategies have become personal to each of us. But somewhere, each of us has learned how to use different strategies and have adopted what works best for each of us in gathering and retaining information.

✓ **Appreciative Listening**

Different from hearing arguments or data heavy content, students also need to understand how to enjoy and to appreciate forms of content, not only in the case of music, art, or literature but in other general interest areas rather than those they are concentrating on in class. Once they have a sense of the structure of what they are hearing, seeing, or reading about, and understand why it might be "good," "highly rated," or "of relatively low value," they can listen or look at content to appreciate its "value" from their own perspective against that backdrop of understanding. In appreciating the material, they make emotional connections with it and form a genuine interest in it or the genre or decide that "it is not for them." The decision they make is not the important part—the process of listening to enjoy or to connect to the material is the definition of appreciative listening.

✓ **Feedback Skills**

Probably the most important parts of collaborative learning or decision-making that are becoming increasingly significant to all students are learning how to determine suitable feedback and how to deliver it. In the Assessment Waterfall Chart (Sharratt & Fullan, 2022; see Figure 4.5), the Descriptive Feedback tier takes time to learn. It is based on several factors including the social/operating norms in the classroom, which talk about "how we will offer feedback" and the co-constructed Success Criteria teachers and students have determined they need to demonstrate because they show the type of content students are striving to produce and against which they should provide feedback to themselves and to their peers.

Figure 4.5 Assessment Waterfall Chart

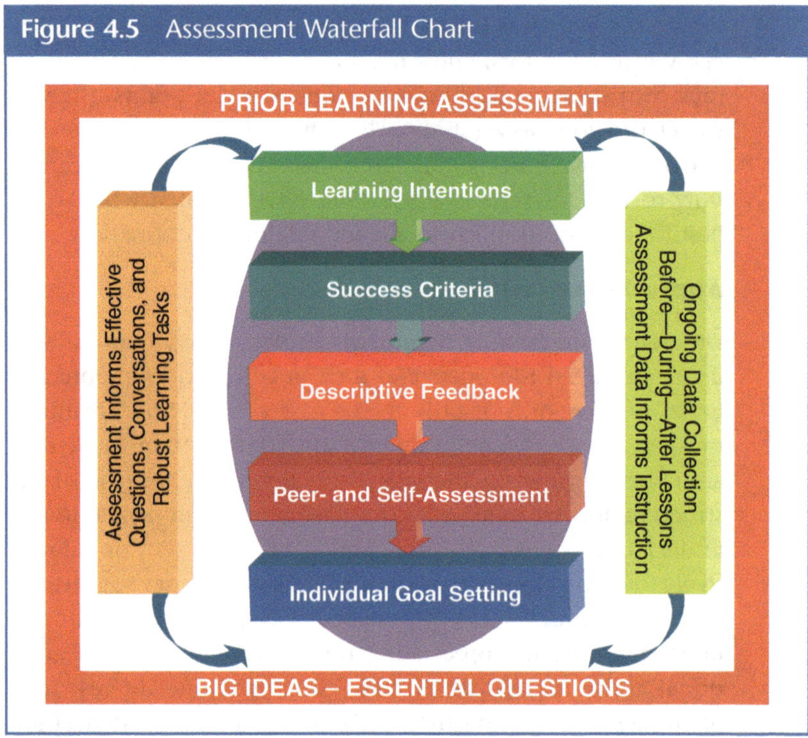

Source: Adapted from York Regional District School Board (2002–2007).

Feedback providers need to ensure they understand what they are assessing, and if they have any questions, they must ask them in order to understand. Importantly, by listening to teachers modeling how to provide feedback, students can become familiar with the necessary thoughtfulness and accuracy against the Success Criteria while still providing an assessment of the content that will enable the other student(s) to learn from the experience.

Providing feedback based on the Success Criteria eliminates or greatly reduces the probability and instances of incorrect feedback, which damages learning of the person whose work is being criticized and the understanding of the task and the learning by the critic. The two pieces of providing feedback then are equally important—understanding the Success Criteria and understanding the student work on the task.

Let's dispense with the argument that Success Criteria are only for K–2 students. Success Criteria when developed with students flow from the Learning Intentions, found in the curriculum expectations and become a defining road map for what success looks like in a unit of work. Teacher and peer feedback is only given against the Success Criteria and that curbs the tendency to give fluffy, inaccurate feedback.

✓ **Nonverbal Communication**

Our students need to learn to look for presenters that fidget, shift from one foot to another, wring hands, develop florid faces, and display overconfident leaning forward into listeners to determine authenticity. While listening to presentations and watching media, nonverbal cues provide another lens into the speaker's meaning and intent. Students must be taught to be very good at "critically consuming" information. They also need to become aware (over time) of other forms of communication, which often are more expressive than the words being used in the presentation.

✓ **Patience and Tolerance**

Self-regulation—specifically within the twin realms of respecting others—and learning to wait for opportunities and for one's turn are part of student maturation beginning in the early years. Yet, having said that, the process can take a great deal longer for some than for others; however, it seems to be a necessarily repetitive process for all students.

Again, the strength of operating norms in each class/school/system is that they create a behavioral contract for listening that contributes to learning both patience and tolerance (and not so coincidentally contributes to greater learning). Equity is a powerful goal for every teacher to instill in the class and across schools and systems; learning tolerance and patience and having them reinforced with agreed-upon rules and standards enables equity.

✓ **Time Management**

Teacher management of class time to provide adequate opportunities for information retrieval and ongoing formative assessments during which students find and process information is a crucial part of class management. Breaking class periods down to provide ten-minute segments of attending, hearing, understanding, appraising, and activating is equal to the effort that the teacher must take in managing the time available and the outcomes wanted from deeply understanding the performance tasks. A more routine class structure will benefit both students who excel at getting started and finished, as well as those who need the structure to keep on track. Learning to manage time becomes a listening skill and a life skill.

✓ **Concentration**

Concentration is maintaining focus on the speaker despite potential distraction and requires eliminating environmental distractions, staying mentally engaged, and practicing mindfulness.

Developing these Attentive Listening skills is a function of classroom management, interpersonal behavior modeled by the teacher, and class operating norms including expectations of personal behavior. These student listening skills contribute to academic success and enhance interpersonal communication and collaboration in various aspects of schooling, school activities, careers after schooling, and life. So, we believe in teaching attentive listening skill sets for students in school. Students can benefit greatly from practicing and refining these skills throughout their educational journey and beyond.

There may be many more expressions of Attentive Listening for students. There can be no question that when teachers engage in Attentive Listening within their classes, they demonstrate all facets they expect students to learn.

✓ **Avoiding Judgment While Listening**

Suspending judgment while listening is critical. This creates a safe space for expression without fear of criticism. *It does not mean* that one will not judge what one has heard; it simply reminds everyone to hear out the discussion or presentation, and having heard—really heard because one has listened thoroughly—then one can begin to analyze and develop a position on the presentation or the issue (I attend, I hear, I understand, I appraise, I activate).

✓ **Cultural Competence**

Recognizing and respecting cultural differences is crucial for effective listening and communication. All should be culturally competent, understanding that others may come from diverse backgrounds with unique communication styles. This has become a vitally important system and school leadership issue, and with good reason, as we have seen before—it can enable or have an enormous negative impact on the learning.

✓ **Adapt-ability**

Being adaptable means adjusting one's listening approach based on the situation and the needs of others. Flexibility in communication styles ensures that diverse learners can effectively engage with others.

✓ **Self-Awareness**

Understanding one's own communication style and biases is a signal that one is self-aware. Self-aware people can actively work on improving their attentive listening skills and creating a more inclusive classroom/school/system environment.

✓ **Active Engagement**

When teachers participate with students during classroom conversations, they both demonstrate and model through verbal and nonverbal cues that they are fully present and attentive.

"Most people do not listen with the intent to understand; they listen with the intent to reply."

—Stephen R. Covey, *The 7 Habits of Highly Effective People: Powerful Lessons in Personal Change.*

DELIBERATE PAUSE

A powerful way to track listening skills in classrooms or in staff meetings is to use a Mind Map. For example, in the classroom, the teacher records the speakers in a student-led forum that is not teacher-directed. Mapping who is talking to whom is a visual way to record who is doing the most listening and the most talking (see Figure 4.6). This Mind Map process gives teachers the data needed to ensure every voice is heard and every voice has an opportunity to build on the ideas of others during conversations—an essential listening skill. This data collection will determine teachers' next steps in developing more equitable participation in classroom, student-directed conversations. A similar mapping tool can be equally effective in staff meetings or professional learning sessions to determine if the format of such meetings allows for listening and talk time to capture all views.

Figure 4.6 Mind Mapping Conversations

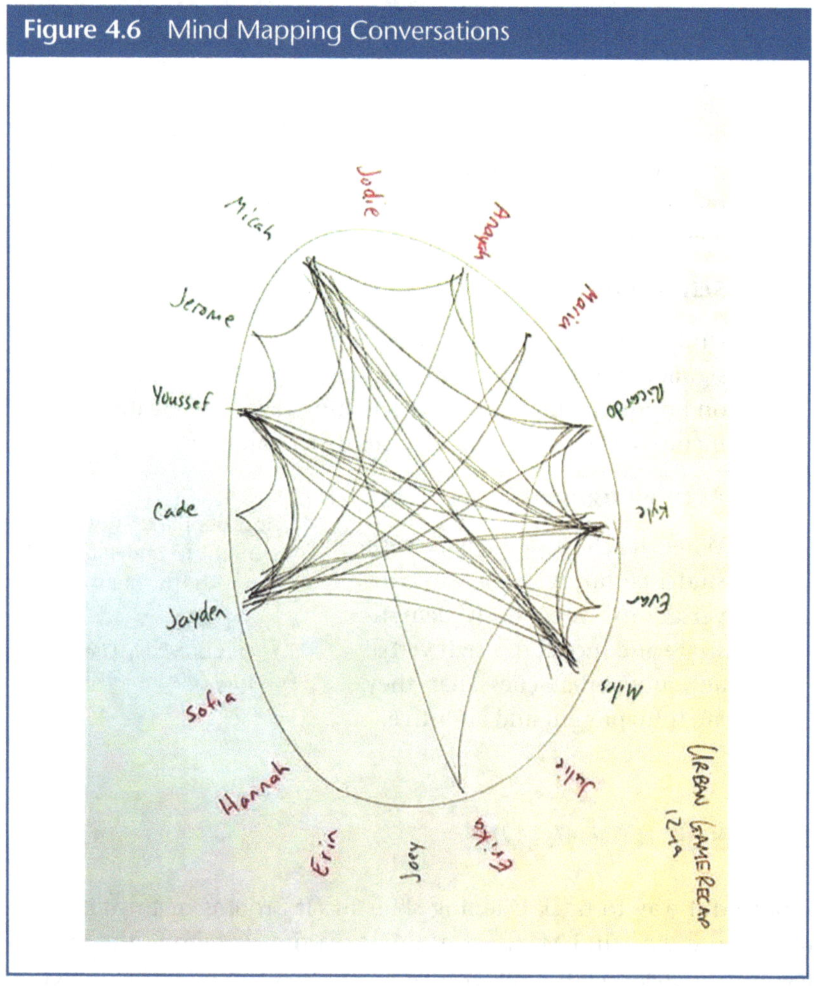

Source: Image by Dr. Lyn Sharratt

In the next chapter, we build on further developing teacher- and student-attentive listening strategies and consider additional practical teaching tools available to teach attentive listening skills. We also consider students' voices in what they believe has helped them become more effective and efficient listeners.

COMMITMENT

I commit to:

1. *Listening to and intently hearing students' voices to inform my practice.*
2. *Investigating what Attentive Listening strategies work best in my (our) classroom(s).*
3. *Teaching students how to discern facts from fiction in conversations.*
4. *Measuring the voices in conversations to determine who can listen to build on the ideas of others.*

LISTENING IN THE CLASSROOM

CHAPTER 5

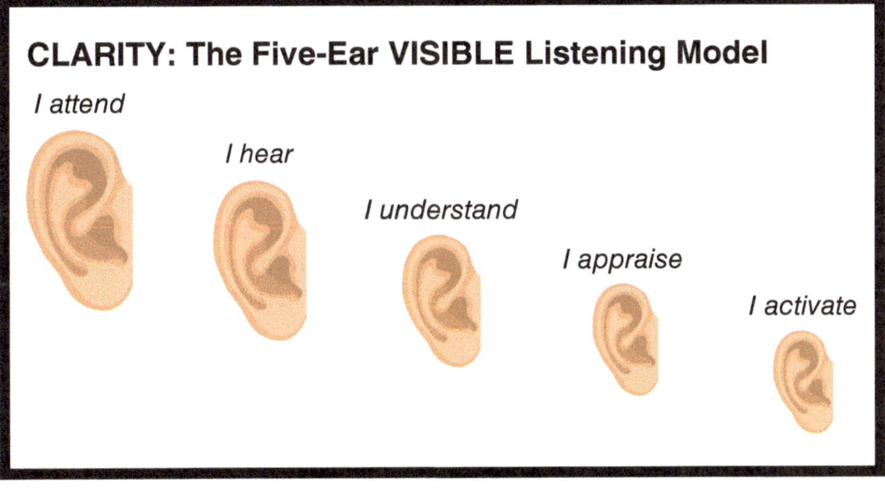

We often avoid teaching students to listen as we believe that learning to listen "just happens." This neglect or forgetfulness demonstrates that listening may be the least understood of the language literacies: the one we contend is the most powerful.

> Listening is the motor for developing strong readers and writers.

Listening must be taught continuously every year from the very early years to the late senior years. The continuously improving learned skills are critical to becoming attentive listeners in tertiary education and in the workforce. As some say, it is why we have two ears and one mouth—we must listen twice as much as we speak to fully comprehend, to ensure those speaking to us present complete messages, and to be able to contribute thoughtfully to the conversation (I attend, I hear, I understand, I appraise, I activate).

As Michelle Sharratt, primary literacy coordinator, York Region District School Board, Ontario, states in personal conversation, June 2024: "It is important for educators to take the time to listen to students in order to deeply understand specific needs and next steps for instruction. But more importantly, strong listening skills show students that you are interested in what they have to say which in turn strengthens the student - educator relationship."

We agree with Sharratt that listening skills should be mapped as a scope and sequence progression from K–12. From this perspective, listening approaches in the classroom refer to the strategies used by teachers to enhance students' listening skills. What we call "attentive listening" is crucial to language acquisition, comprehension, and overall academic success. Therefore, listening must be modeled and taught by teachers who create a safe space for change in perspective and learning growth in their classrooms and lessons. Here are some common listening approaches that are used in classrooms and have been proven to be impactful when considered together and are seen as relevant for K–12 students:

- ✓ **Prior Learning Assessment (PLA).** Unpacking PLA and building background information ensure that students have enough context, background knowledge, and vocabulary to make the learning meaningful. "Known commonly as top-down processing, the use of prior knowledge assists listeners in constructing interpretations that are complete and meaningful. Top-down processing can help listeners bridge gaps in comprehension and construct a reasonable interpretation without depending too much on linguistic features (Izumi, 2003). Activating prior knowledge can be generated from "parallel activities" (e.g. reading, viewing) that accompany a listening event, such as attending a lecture. Flowerdew and Miller (2005, p. 90) refer to this as the "intertextual dimension" of comprehension. Prior knowledge facilitates quicker processing. Tyler (2001) found that when listeners had access to the topic, differences in working memory consumption between native and "experienced" non-native listeners were not statistically significant. Top-down processing is clearly important; however, learners sometimes miss opportunities to apply prior knowledge because their attention is focused entirely on trying to decode and parse the speech stream." (Vandergrift & Goh, 2009, p. 4)

✓ **Literacy Learning.** Most impactful is teaching listening behaviors with the language skills of listening, speaking, phonics, phonological awareness, reading, writing, viewing, and representing in all content areas. Listening is often a neglected area of literacy instruction, K–12. It **begins** with learning to listen and **becomes** listening to learn and think critically and **is evidenced by** the Gradual Release and Acceptance of Responsibility (GR/AR) model (adapted from Vygotsky, 1978). GR/AR works effectively in any subject area or grade level. Specific listening instruction that is scaffolded, using the GR/AR model, helps learners discover, rehearse, and apply listening processes. GR/AR allows teachers to differentiate instruction and flexibly group students with like needs for instruction, changing up groups on an ongoing basis and using in-class assessment data to inform decision-making. The scaffolding process for instructional support involves gradually reducing assistance:

It begins with the full support given in modeling, decreases support in sharing, provides minimal guidance, and eventually offers only availability to assist students as they become independent. Finally, no support is provided as the student develops the ability to apply new knowledge independently. The Gradual Release and Acceptance of Responsibility model reinforces the importance of class management, especially establishing classroom routines. We acknowledge that "one size doesn't fit all" and this model ensures a gradual release of the ownership of learning. Releasing the learning to students and having them accept new knowledge creation will occur at differing rates depending on students' readiness and capacity to listen and accept that learning. Many high impact listening strategies—some discussed in this chapter—support this approach and accomplish the differentiation of instruction demanded and expected in classrooms today to meet the diverse learning needs of all students, K–12.

The GR/AR model moves through a continuum of *five* carefully planned scaffolds from high to low teacher support (Sharratt, 2019), allowing and facilitating differentiation of instruction for learners as illustrated in figure 5.1):

Modeled Practice: Teachers explicitly model proficient listening and thinking behaviors through "think-alouds," while students listen and watch attentively. This includes modeling attentive listening while maintaining eye contact, nodding, and responding appropriately where there is the highest teacher support while students listen.

Shared Practice: Teachers and students practice the GR/AR approach together, listening to each other. The student gradually assumes more and more responsibility for their learning and the balance begins to change to a lower level of teacher support.

Guided Practice: Students practice the skill or behavior with explicit coaching questions from the teacher to construct meaning, often at a quiet table in the classroom for guided support. Students listen and return quickly to do the assigned work related to the skill/behavior practiced in the guided group. Specific feedback is offered to individual or small groups of learners during the guided stage, practicing or reteaching a concept with the teacher.

Independent Practice: Students practice the skill/behavior independently within the classroom context and receive teacher and peer feedback, taking ownership of their new learning and having opportunities to listen and talk accountably with classmates. The teacher's role shifts to being very engaged in this component of GR/AR as facilitators of small group and individual student conferences to ensure Attentive Listening leads to attending, hearing, understanding, appraising and activating.

Learner Application: Students apply previously taught skills to new genres of discussion and listening, new formats, more difficult texts, or in other disciplines, demonstrating a transfer of the learning to a new situation. By attending, hearing, and understanding, students can question and gain clarification in order to articulate clearly their thoughts and ideas about the new learning—they appraise and activate—and the ownership of their learning overtakes the teacher's input in this final stage.

It is important that teachers plan for and follow the full GR/AR model. Many "model" and then move swiftly to the independent stage, for example doing a hundred questions on a concept, without planning to share the learning, without guiding the learning or even, supporting independent learning and taking students into applying the learning in different contexts. In any given classroom across all subject areas, there should be groups of students at each of these levels simultaneously. When the GR/AR teaching model is used, thinking aloud, encouraging risk-taking, scaffolding, coaching and guiding, feedback, and concluding with reflection become "habits of mind" for learners. Ultimately, this approach to learning encourages students to listen and to assess what is being heard (I activate) so that they become assessment-capable (Frey et al., 2018) and know the expected next steps to their own learning.

Figure 5.1 The Gradual Release and Acceptance of Responsibility

Source: Reprinted from Sharratt, 2018.

Figure 5.1 (Sharratt, 2019) demonstrates the GR/AR learning progressions when each of the above five stages of development is intentionally planned so that students' learning-to-listen is scaffolded over time. Unfortunately, the Gradual Release learning progression is not lock-step; it is scaffolded to meet individual student needs, determined by the teacher. Thus, students will work in small groups on like skills and move in and out of these staged groups flexibly, as determined by self or teacher assessment against the Success Criteria as demonstrated in figure 5.2. We note here that Listening is the silent thinking ingredient that must be present in every component of the Assessment Waterfall Chart. Surely this Gradual Release/Acceptance of Responsibility approach is the art and science of teaching when listening is the foundational, assumed component (Figure 5.2)

Figure 5.2 Assessment Waterfall Chart

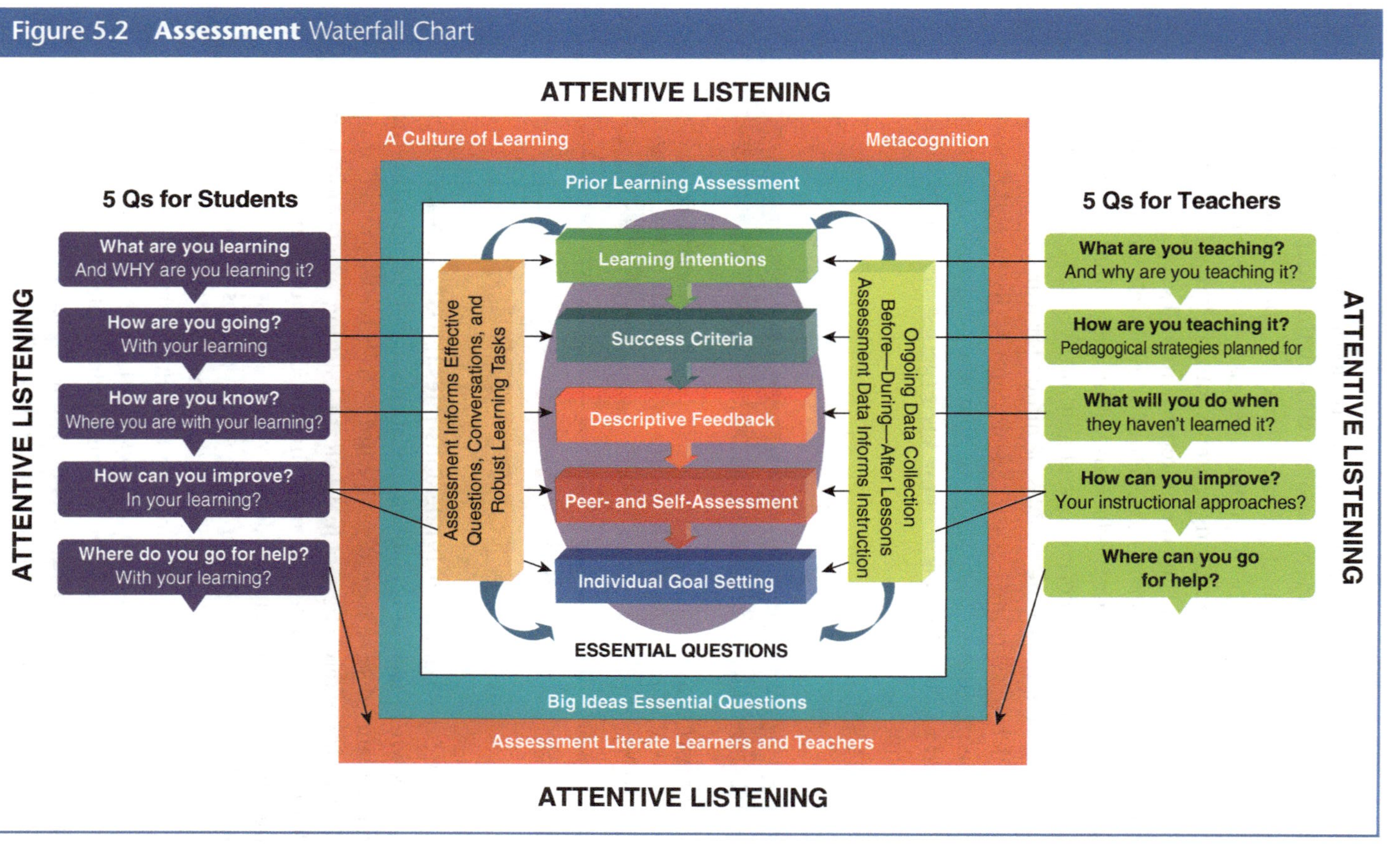

Source: Created by the Diocese of Lismore Catholic Schools. Used with permission.

- ✓ **Real-World Listening.** We have access to so many modalities of texts. It is important that students listen to a variety of carefully selected, authentic materials such as podcasts, news reports, interviews, webinars and videos, to name just a few. These materials expose students to real-life language, accents, and various communication styles. Incorporating technology tools, such as educational apps, interactive websites, or multimedia presentations, makes listening exercises more engaging and interactive for students. However, there must be a relevant purpose for the listening and a visible and assessable outcome or artifact of learning resulting from the listening (Figure 5.3).

Figure 5.3 Visual Anchor Chart Connecting Listening and Speaking to Assessment Literacy

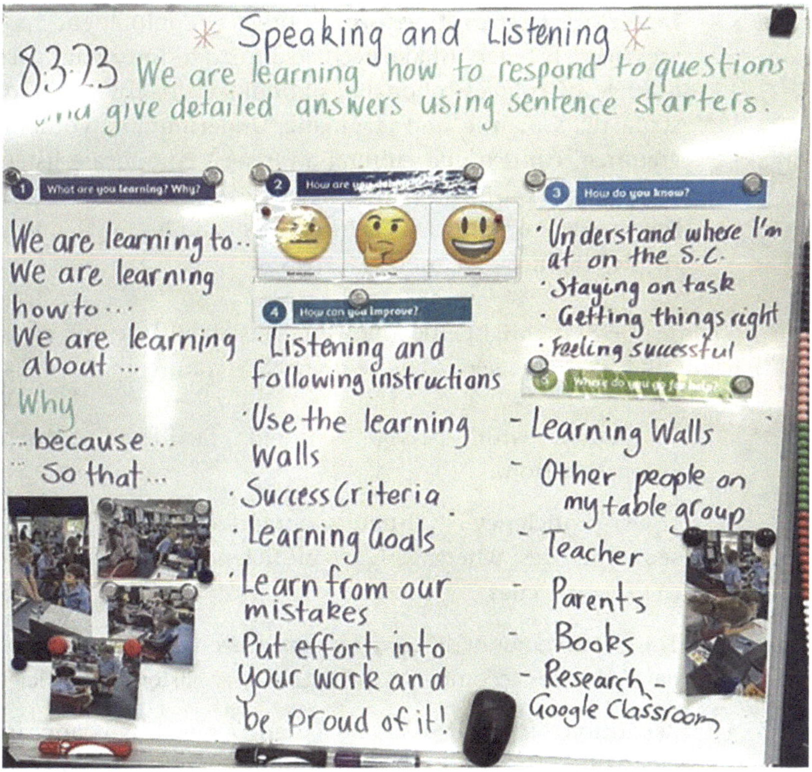

Source: Created by Michelle Sharratt. Used with permission.

- ✓ **Assessment Tools.** Tools for listening include specific Learning Intentions and Success Criteria (Figure 5.3), quizzes, oral presentations, or discussions based on the information heard, which then provide opportunities for descriptive feedback on students' listening skills.
- ✓ **Comprehension Cues.** Teachers must demonstrate listening cues, in order to show students what responsive listeners do and what they, as students, need to emulate. Involved listeners give minimal responses or cues to what is being said, such as "Hmmm, yeah, OK, right, I see, head nods". Minimal responses mean that they don't interrupt the flow of dialogue. When these short vocalizations, glances, and facial expressions (e.g., smiles) are missing, the speaker assumes a negative reaction. Such feedback, called 'providing back-channeling cues', is a significant part of the body language of listening.
- ✓ **Listening Comprehension.** In order to comprehend spoken messages, listeners (may) need to integrate information from a range of sources: phonetic, phonological, prosodic, lexical, syntactic, semantic, and pragmatic. Understanding vocabulary, grammar, context and cultural awareness complicate listening comprehension. The fact that we achieve all this in real time as the message unfolds makes listening "complex, dynamic, and fragile" (Berne, 1998, in Osada, p. 56).

Berne (1998) highlights the following facts about listening comprehension that have emerged from the research literature:

- ✓ Familiarity with passage content facilitates . . . listening comprehension.
- ✓ Lower-proficiency . . . listeners attend to phonological or semantic cues, whereas higher-proficiency . . . listeners attend to semantic cues.
- ✓ The effectiveness of different types of speech modifications or visual aids varies according to the degree of . . . listening proficiency.
- ✓ Repetition of passages should be encouraged as it appears to facilitate . . . listening comprehension more than other types of modifications.

- ✓ The use of pre-listening activities, particularly those that provide short synopses of the listening passage to follow or allow listeners to preview the comprehension questions, facilitate . . . listening comprehension.
- ✓ The use of videotape, as opposed to audiotape, as a means of presenting listening passages facilitates . . . listening comprehension, especially with regard to attitudinal and attentional factors.
- ✓ The use of authentic, as opposed to pedagogical, listening passages leads to greater improvement in . . . listening comprehension performance.
- ✓ Training in the use of listening strategies facilitates . . . listening comprehension and . . . learners can and should be taught how to use listening strategies.
- ✓ Due to the complex nature of listening comprehension, . . . listening practice should encompass a wide range of situations where listening is required as well as different types of listening, different types of listening passages, different modes of presentation (e.g., live, videotape, audiotape), and different types of activities or tasks (Berne, 1998, in Osada, p. 56).

Despite gaps between theory and practice, listening comprehension can be developed and strengthened over time through planned, consistent practice. For example,

- ✓ Asking clarifying questions to enhance understanding is a "must-do" modeling strategy for every teacher to use.
- ✓ Having students paraphrase or restate information in their own words confirms comprehension.
- ✓ Teaching notetaking, like jotting down main points of a lesson or concept can compensate for memory constraints.
- ✓ Accountable Talk (further explained below).

Listening and Speaking are inextricably linked. By co-constructing Operating Norms focused on expected listening behaviors, and modeling what Accountable Talk looks and sounds like for speakers, listeners, and responders, teachers serve the instrumental role of creating and establishing a safe, responsive learning environment in which students can practice listening and speaking. Teachers model, unpack, and display their listening operating norms (how we will treat each other) and protocols (how we will progress turn-taking, justifications, and academic controversy in conversations) as visual cues for learners. Teachers have students practice these strategies as listeners and as speakers in a dialogue or group discussion, so they know how to own and present their own thoughts and learning, and how to reflect on and respond graciously to the thoughts presented by their classmates. This is Accountable Talk (Sharratt, 2019). Figure 5.4 outlines "Accountable Talk Stems" that should be prominently displayed and used in every K–12 classroom. Accountable Listening becomes Accountable Talking.

Figure 5.4 Accountable Talk Discussion Starters

Sample Accountable Talk Phrases That Promote Thinking:

- Tell me more about . . .
- Is there another way to say that, Audrey?
- Can you build on Jackson's idea?
- Is there an example that explains what you are thinking, Ryan?
- What is your evidence to defend your thinking, Aeson?
- Why do you agree with that point of view, Clarke?
- I agree with Robbie, and I also think . . .
- That's a great idea, Penelope, and I would add . . .
- I disagree with Madeleine's point (not Madeleine) because . . .

Source: Reprinted from Sharratt, 2019.

A substantial portion of instructional time involves students talking about developing concepts, big ideas, and essential questions. To facilitate an impactful working/learning environment, teachers use instructional processes such as academic controversy (outlined below), panel discussions, literature circles, case study exploration, mock trials, conferences, podcasts, presentations, interviews, debates, and so forth. Attentive listening is involved in each of these interactive Accountable Talk strategies.

We have stated before and because it is so vitally important, we want to restate what Mathieson (2007) proposes. To create a classroom environment that builds learning power, a teacher must develop positive interpersonal relationships, honor student voice, and encourage perspective-taking. Teachers can nurture Accountable Talk by further developing their culture of learning and promoting an open-to-learning stance in the classroom. In such an environment all responses are accepted, all students are respected, and mistakes are treated as rich opportunities to learn content and develop personal styles to apply their learning. In this type of classroom culture getting started on a project and Failing Fast are more highly regarded than is delaying the start and possibly still failing when it is too late to repair the project or response.

In a culture of learning, students learn from each other through the virtuous cycle of newly developing Attentive Listening techniques that subsequently develop into Accountable Talk which further improve learned listening techniques. While the Learning Intention may be building specific new knowledge together so that all students flourish, a key element of the Success Criteria is demonstrating continuously improving listening skills. **Literacy learning that leads to critical literacy is the complex interaction of skills, resources, listening behaviors, and "thinking aloud" that propel students to think critically and creatively.**

DELIBERATE PAUSE

Academic Controversy (AC) is a classroom listening strategy that provides an opportunity to hear, reflect, and respond to differing perspectives on important issues inside and outside the classroom. AC must be structured to hearing others' viewpoints, to being open to learning new concepts and ideas, and to changing mindsets.

OPERATING NORMS

It is critical to co-construct with the class or to remind the class of the Operating Norms before engaging in this activity *to encourage* risk-taking interaction, that is, "Failing Fast," or trying something new. Some sample Operating Norms might include the following:

- ✓ Listen to *all* perspectives
- ✓ Be respectful
- ✓ Disagree agreeably
- ✓ Don't personalize comments
- ✓ Be open to new ideas
- ✓ Change your mind through attentive listening and reflective thinking
- ✓ *Build on the ideas of others to achieve the best solution.*

PROTOCOL

Form groups of three to four students to do the following:

- ✓ Define the issue or problem and identify the two positions: This can be teacher directed to begin but should morph into student initiated.
- ✓ Assign each team a unique position.
- ✓ Groups research their position and articulate the main ideas and details to persuade the other groups to adopt their position.
- ✓ Questions go back and forth among the groups, facilitated by the teacher.
- ✓ Groups exchange perspectives then summarize the others' positions.

To conclude, groups come together to state a consensus position, based on information and perspectives of each group. For the assessment task, students write an individual opinion as to which position they support, and if they changed positions, justify why that was the case. Then, a "congress," or whole class sharing time of individual positions taken, occurs when students have an opportunity to refer back to the Success Criteria achieved during this unit of study.

Listening to each other and talking accountably creates vibrant learning communities that explode with excitement about learning! In the next chapter, we will explore voices in the classroom to hear students' thinking that builds on listening to each other.

COMMITMENT

I commit to:

1. *Listening to and intently hearing students' voices to inform my practice.*
2. *Understanding and embedding the research findings that point to the power of Accountable Talking and Listening as a pillar of quality teaching in every classroom.*
3. *Experimenting with new approaches to promote efficient listening among my students.*

LISTENING TO VOICES

Who Is Doing the Most Listening, Talking, Interpreting, and Thinking?

CHAPTER 6

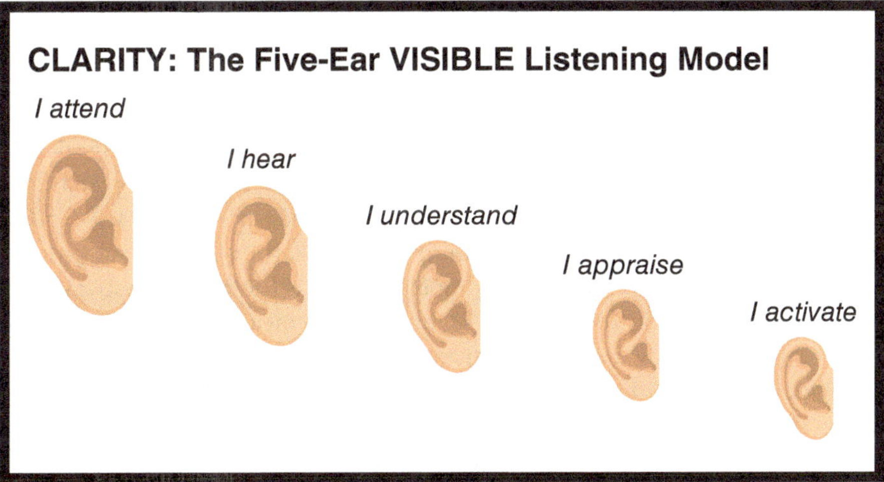

We wrote about the power of Accountable Talk in the previous chapter, but wait a minute, there can be no Accountable Talk without Accountable Listening! They are two sides of the same coin!

Video: Rich Classroom Discussions in Math

https://bit.ly/46ZkNed

Video: Encouraging Academic Conversations With Talk Moves

https://bit.ly/49AUb44

Video: How to Use Accountable Talk

https://bit.ly/3XjE4DN

PDF: "Having Grand Conversations in the Classroom," Ontario Ministry of Education (2011)

https://bit.ly/3yVtedQ

Accountable Talk and Accountable Listening together contribute to *building the structural capacity* within an individual's Oral Language development. While these skills are so critical in early years' learning (Sharratt, 2019, Chapter 5), they *become essential* in creating new knowledge for people of any age. We learn from others. Learning is a social process (Bandura, 1986). **Talk**, speaking effectively, is the single most valuable indicator of our thinking, our ability to make meaning and understanding, of assessing our own learning and that of our students. However, the power of talk to precisely convey meaning is **derived from effective listening**, from every step in the Five Ear Listening Model: attending, hearing, understanding, appraising, and activating the newly gained knowledge.

Learning to express oneself literately is difficult enough (and stressful enough) in one-on-one conversations with a teacher or a mentor; however, that stress is multiplied dramatically when one is asked to spontaneously express a thought to a group of peers without having had time to think it through, to listen and watch for feedback cues, or to "talk it out" in those situations (Sharratt, 2019). Even having to read aloud one's previously written personal thoughts is incredibly stressful if one hasn't had an opportunity to discuss them and receive some form of feedback from someone else. Listening is as critical to the expression of thinking as is *talking* to the expression of thinking. *Two sides of the same coin.*

Effective teachers and leaders create communities of conversationalists when members of the community—students and teacher—are guided and protected by protocols that reduce anxiety. This protection and encouragement enables students to test out their ideas and learn new things alongside their peers. Putting these protocols in place causes a "deliberate pause" for teachers and leaders, to ask themselves and learn to monitor, **"Who is doing the most thinking, listening, interpreting and the most talking in our classrooms and in our Professional Learning (PL) conversations?"** In each case, the balance between "Student-listening-to teacher talking" in classrooms and "teacher-listening-to leader talking" in Professional Learning sessions must tip the scales outweighing every instance of teachers or leaders "talking-at" learners in classes or colleagues during PL sessions.

> "When people talk, listen completely. Most people never listen."
>
> —Ernest Hemingway

Why is it important to create communities of conversationalists? Reading and writing and presenting a point of view verbally must always begin with talking about one's thinking with someone else such as a "talk partner." Learners, from young learners to graduate students and adults participating in PL appreciate and become much more competent in presenting their thinking when they have opportunities for oral rehearsal (listening and talking) as a first step before being called upon to answer.

Accountable Listening and Talking are **data collection tools** for classroom teachers answering the questions: "What do my students know?"; "Can they make the links between the big ideas?"; "What do they need to know next?"; "What do I need to know to move my students forward?"; and "What do I need to reteach in a different way (not louder and longer in the same way)?". Accountable Listening and Talking are **learning tools** for students who ask themselves: "What do I know?"; "What do I want to learn?"; "How will I learn it?"; "Who can I talk to in order to clarify and extend my thinking?" These are certainly the same questions that leaders should ask when planning staff PL sessions, and that teaching staff can ask themselves and others as they think about their learning needs.

In this chapter, we unpack the meaning of Accountable Listening and Talking; offer a strong research base of evidence that recommends using both; describe the practical application of Accountable Listening and Talking in the classroom with students and during Professional Learning (PL) sessions for teachers and leaders together; and, in conclusion, we listen to students and consider what Accountable Listening and Talking look like in a secondary context.

WHAT IS ACCOUNTABLE LISTENING AND TALKING?

The term "Accountable Listening and Talking" in classrooms refers to talk that is meaningful, respectful, and mutually beneficial to both speaker and listener because, on the one hand, it sharpens the listener's understanding of what is being heard, and on the other hand, it enables a sharpening of the concept being expressed. Note, it does not imply agreement with the concept. It does, however, ensure the speaker and listener both understand the concept. Accountable Listening and Talking stimulates higher-order thinking—helping students to learn, reflect on their learning, and communicate their knowledge and understanding. To promote Accountable Listening and Talking, teachers create collaborative learning environments (The Third Teacher, Sharratt, 2019, pp. 9–10) in which students feel confident expressing their ideas, opinions, and knowledge (Ontario Ministry of Education, 2004).

ACCOUNTABLE LISTENING AND TALKING HAS A STRONG RESEARCH BASE

Accountable Listening and Talking as a critical way to bring learners' voices into focus is steeped in research. Some of the available research studies substantiate the importance of students' verbalizing their thinking in classrooms while seeking to hear reciprocal questions and affirmations.

1. Sharratt (1996), discussed the four levels of discourse/talk that begin with purposeful listening:

   Discussion: lowest level and often quick as a decision needs to be made;

Dialogue: higher level because there is no expectation that a decision must be made so conversation flows more easily;

Reflection: high level as more time is taken to *retell* your thinking, *relate* it to what has already occurred, and end with *reflection* on what is possible. *Retell, relate, reflect* is a higher-order thinking framework that demands listening (Sharratt, 2019 pp. 161–162);

Silence: is often an indicator that ideas are being formulated, making meaning is being investigated, and new knowledge is being created. This is when teachers must resist rushing in to rescue students. *Wait-time is a virtue; waiting for a time is virtuous.* It is ok to let students struggle and "talk it through" before expecting a "correct" answer as that struggle is often the best time for their/our brains to work. Teachers need to be attuned to silence and determine why students are being silent—are they thinking or not understanding or disengaged?

2. The research of Michaels et al. (2008) about academically productive classroom talk suggests that the critical features of classroom talk fall under three broad dimensions: accountability to the learning community, accountability to the knowledge, and accountability to accepted standards of reasoning. **All are underpinned by effective, active listening skills**. For example:

   ✓ **Accountable to the Learning Community**

   This is talk that attends (listens) seriously to and builds on the ideas of other participants and provides cues to each other. Students ask each other questions aimed at clarifying, sharpening understanding, and/or expanding a proposition.

   ✓ **Accountable to the Knowledge**

   This is talk that is based explicitly on facts, written texts, or other publicly accessible information that all individuals can access. Students make an effort to get their facts right and make explicit the evidence behind their claims or explanation. Still, there are interpretations of specific knowledge, whether new questions are provoked or further questions are asked to address the implications of the facts being discussed.

- ✓ **Accountable to the Accepted Standards of Reasoning (Rigorous Thinking)**

  This is talk that emphasizes logical connections and the drawing of reasonable conclusions. It is talk that involves explanation and self-correction. It often involves searching for new or extensions to existing premises, rather than simply supporting or attacking conclusions. It demands creating a thorough understanding within the community of conversationalists.

3. Mathieson (2007) proposes that in order to create a learning environment that builds learning power, a teacher must create positive interpersonal relationships, honor student voice, and encourage perspective-taking. Similarly, teachers can also nurture Accountable Listening and Talking by fostering a culture of learning and promoting an "open-to-learning" stance in the classroom where all responses are heard and accepted, all students are respected, and mistakes are treated as rich opportunities for learning (Sharratt, 2019).

4. West (2012) states that only when you make students' thinking visible on classroom walls, can you hear what they are thinking and give accurate feedback.

5. A research monograph produced by the Ontario Ministry of Education (2011) summarizes many research studies by stating, "When teachers open up a conversation that allows students to take the lead, the classroom becomes a place where learning from one another is the norm, not the exception. Involving students in collaborative structures and teaching students how to engage in [listen to] meaningful conversations . . . makes a difference in student learning and achievement, supporting the development of the higher order thinking skills which are so critical to today's learners."

PROFESSIONAL LEARNING FOR TEACHERS AND LEADERS MUST MODEL "ACCOUNTABLE LISTENING AND TALKING" MOVES IN THE CLASSROOM

Professional Learning for teachers and leaders must reflect/model good classroom practice. By co-constructing operating norms and modeling what Accountable Listening and Talking look and sound like for speakers, listeners, and responders, PL leaders serve the instrumental role in modeling and reinforcing what it looks like to create and firmly establish the "Third Teacher" and culture of learning in every PL classroom (Sharratt, 2019, pp. 9–10). The following are some key "Listening and Talking Moves" to ensure ongoing dialogue during every PL session and which teachers attending the PL should be expected to replicate in their classrooms.

1. **Co-construct Operating Norms.** Operating Norms that are established for PL sessions should be similar to those that teachers and students would co-construct. In studying Accountable Listening and Talking, we would expect to develop the following Operating Norms:

   - Listening to others
   - Hearing every voice
   - Building on the ideas of others
   - Disagreeing agreeably
   - Changing my beliefs and understanding given the evidence presented
   - Practicing sentence stems, such as: "I agree with Dr. Johnston and would add . . ."; I disagree with what Dr. Johnston is saying because . . ."; Based on my evidence, I think . . ."; I can clarify what I mean by . . ."
   - Encouraging others; cheering for others' successes

   We benefit from the strengths of all when we encourage peers to contribute their thinking in our learning communities. In focusing on Accountable Listening and Talking, we must use Operating Norms and refer to them often to establish an environment of safety and trust, not only during PL sessions but later when doing Learning Walks & Talks in classrooms where we should find Operating Norms evident—that is in all classrooms.

   Itzchakov et al. (2024) noted that particularly during disagreements, we find it difficult to listen particularly when the views being talked about are inconsistent with our views. But when we experience the other talkers showing high-quality listening, then we engage more openly and less defensively, often leading to gaining insights about the others' attitudes and viewpoints. Such "good listening" involves "maintaining eye contact, asking relevant follow-up and clarifying questions, displaying nonverbal cues that convey attentiveness" and nodding and eye contact, while avoiding external and internal distractions (p. 2).

2. **Establish an "Open-to-Learning Stance."** We invite risk-taking, participation, and inquiry when we invite others to share their thinking by proposing they "say more about that." For example, teachers and leaders in all learning-focused sessions use and model the following:

   - attentive listening,
   - think-alouds,
   - participation prompts,
   - leading conversations, and
   - justifications of proposals and challenges.

   During PL with groups and individuals, teachers and leaders have learners practice these strategies, so they know how to own and present their own thoughts and how to reflect on and respond graciously to the thoughts presented by their peers. This is "Accountable Listening and Accountable Talking-in-Action." It is only by practicing these skills and becoming both proficient and comfortable with them that it becomes possible to migrate the behavior into classrooms.

3. **Model Attentive Listening.** Listening is an active meaning-making process that requires explicit instruction, time, practice, and commitment. Teachers [leaders] need time to sit alongside students [teachers] to listen-in to their thinking to understand where the students [teachers] are and then, accountably speak with them to help them clarify their thoughts and check for understanding. Monitoring one's own ability to listen, contribute, and build on ideas rather than impatiently waiting for one's turn to speak is critical to exposing and supporting student thinking (Meikle, 2016, Blog).

4. **Commit to Assessment "for" and "as" Learning.** Developing understanding of the Assessment Waterfall Chart (AWC) below (CLARITY, 2019, p. 124) provides another opportunity to embrace Accountable Listening and Talking. Through co-constructing the meaning of every component part, everyone learns the AWC process and through their verbal input everyone demonstrates they are learning the underlying meaning of every step of the Assessment-Instruction Waterfall Chart (as assessment and instruction are two sides of the same coin). This is a process not only with teachers in PL and often in subsequent interactions with leaders but also with teachers when co-planning units and, of course, with students in classrooms.

PRACTICAL APPLICATION OF ACCOUNTABLE LISTENING AND TALKING IN CLASSROOM PRACTICE

A substantial portion of instructional time must involve students in listening and talking, which is related to developing concepts, big ideas, and essential questions that surround the Instruction Waterfall Chart above (Sharratt, 2019, chapter 5, Figure 5.2). To do this, teachers use the powerful Accountable Listening and Talking **approach**. The monograph "Having Grand Conversations" (2011) elaborates on several Accountable Listening and Talking strategies that can be heard in K–12 classrooms in every subject area across the globe. The following are a few of the most powerful:

1. Allow Appropriate Think Time/Wait Time

Research conducted on the pacing of questions shows the average amount of time a teacher waits between posing a question and eliciting a response (think time gap) is less than one second (Rowe, 1986). This gap must increase to enable students to listen, then talk about what they think with another student before being called on to answer. With only one-second wait time, students' answers were reported to be very short (five seconds on average) and less than three words seventy percent of

Figure 6.1 The **Instruction** Waterfall Chart

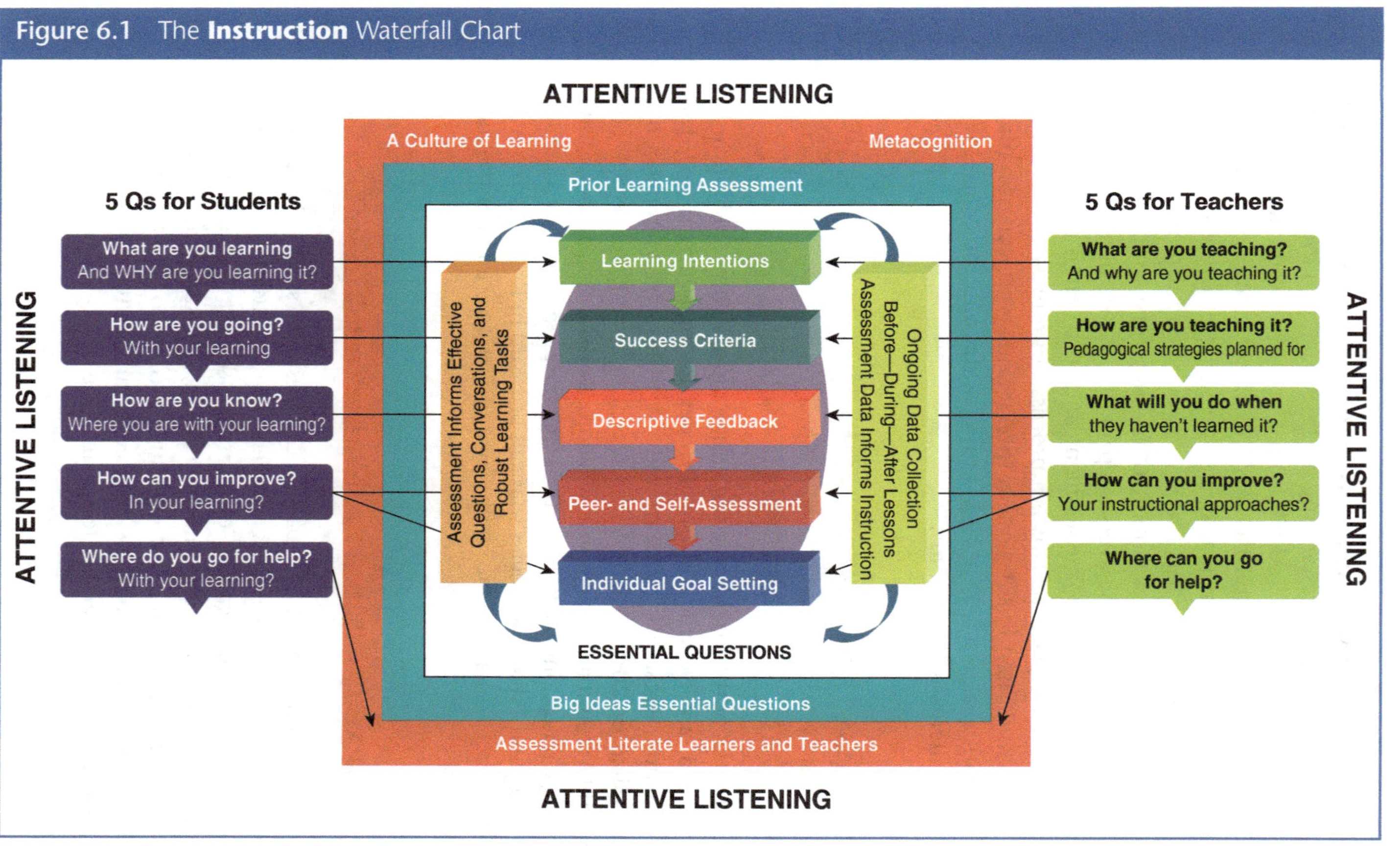

Source: Adapted from York Regional District School Board (2002–2007).

the time (Alexander, 2001). The addition of a minimum of three seconds of "think time" has been shown to improve the quality of student responses and learning. (refer to Questioning Viewer Guide, Learning Video Series: www.edugains.ca).

2. Use Think-Pair-Share and Turn and Talk

Think-Pair-Share and Turn and Talk are designed to promote and support higher-order thinking. The teacher asks students to think about a specific topic, pair with another student to listen, discuss their thinking, and finally share their collaboratively structured ideas with the group. The teacher will want to give students enough time to permit in-depth conversation. Too much time given to students for sharing permits them to go off-topic or to lose interest. Professional judgment and careful observation (listening) are needed to determine the quality of the generated responses. To increase individual accountability and student confidence, the teacher could also have students write or diagram their answers after thinking and before sharing (Questioning Viewer Guide, Learning Video Series: www.edugains.ca).

3. Encourage Student-Designed Higher-Order Thinking (HOT) Questions

University of Melbourne researcher Dr. Janet Clinton found that, on average, teachers asked about two hundred questions per day, while students each asked two questions per week about their work, leaving out procedural questions such as "what page am I supposed to be on." Possibly the more interesting issue exposed than the number of questions asked is that "high achieving" students are OK with this paucity of questions. They can weed through what is essential and what is not on their own, while struggling students, on the other hand, want the teacher to stop, so they can talk it out with a peer who can explain it to them in more student-friendly language (DeWitt, 2020).

Strategies like using a Q-chart or KWLN chart (We **Know** – We **Wonder** – We **Learned** – What's **New**) example below, or a display of "Question Starters" help students generate questions that make them active participants in Listening and Learning Conversations.

Figure 6.2 Unpacking Student Knowledge Before and After a Unit

Name: Date:

Topic: *American Revolution War*

1. Jot down what you know about this topic in column 1. Number these things.
2. Think about what else you want to know about what you listed in column 1 and write those questions in column 2. Number your questions so they match the numbers in column 1.
3. Read about the topics. If you found answers to your questions, write those in column 3.
4. If you found new information, write that in column 4.

What do I know?	What do I want to know?	What answers did I learn?	What did I learn that's new?
1. It was to have independence	1. Why did it have to be a war? →	1. Because British didn't agree to representation for taxation	1775–1783 George Washington was Commander-in-Chief
	1. Was everyone here for it? →	1. Loyalists said don't split from Crown.	
2. It was against England →	2. How did they know we wanted independence? →	2. Sent list of grievances	

What do I know?	What do I want to know?	What answers did I learn?	What did I learn that's new?
3. There was the Boston Tea party →	3. What was it? →	3. Not a party! People snuck on ship and threw tea in Boston Harbor. Made British mad and they made Intolerable Acts and that made colonists mad and that started war	No regular army + not even uniforms First shot in Lexington, Massachusetts. Battle of Saratoga is turning point. British army better prepared.
4. Paul ____ rode his horse →	4. What do people talk about him? →	4. Solve myth. Warned that British were coming	
5. We won! →	5. ?		
6. We have the 4th of July because we won.	6. Who invented the firecracker? →	6. ?	
6. Declaration of independence was agreed to on July 4th, 1776, but war wasn't over until 1783. We celebrate the signing			

(Continued)

(Continued)

Q-Chart Questions	Is	Did	Can	Will	Would	Might	Should
Who							
What		Knowledge				Predict	
Where							
When							
Why		Analytical				Synthesis	
How							

4. Create Rich Tasks

In order for the students to begin using Accountable Listening and Talking there must be interesting, complex ideas and rich, robust tasks to listen to and argue about that require teachers to move away from simple questions and one-word answers to problems that support multiple positions or solution paths (Michaels et al., 2008). Rich Tasks build on a knowledge framework and ask students to consider what the task is asking, how to solve the task, what strategies to use, what processes are needed, and how to explain their reasoning (West, 2011). Rich Tasks demand Accountable Listening and Talking through partner-small-and whole-group sharing in a risk-free learning environment. Figure 6.3 displays questions teachers ask themselves when planning Rich Tasks for students.

Figure 6.3 Self-Assessment of a Robust Performance Task

Key Questions to Ask When Planning a Robust Performance Task

- Is there a clear link between the Learning Intentions from the curriculum expectations and the task that students are expected to do to demonstrate their learning?
- Is there evidence of the big ideas and essential questions being asked?
- Are the students involved in the co-construction of the Success Criteria they will use to self-assess their performance task?
- Is there an opportunity to give Descriptive Feedback linked to the Success Criteria?
- Does the task demand Accountable Talk through partner and small group work?
- Is the text selection suitable to the age and ability of the learners?
- Are there different entry levels for different learners?
- Does the task require higher-order thinking, reading, and writing?
- Is there an opportunity to scaffold the learning for each student?
- Is the task relevant to students' lives?
- Will it allow the students to demonstrate the Success Criteria to achieve the highest level of performance—an "A," for example?

Source: Reprinted from Sharratt, 2018.

5. Even More!

Additional Accountable Listening and Talking strategies that are detailed in the "Having Grand Conversations" Monograph (Ontario Ministry of Education, 2011) include the following:

1. Panel discussions
2. Literature circles
3. Case study exploration
4. Presentations, interviews, debates
5. Inside-outside circles
6. Fishbowl, and
7. "Say Something"

Changing up or variably using the many Accountable Listening and Talking strategies stretches thinking and allows receptivity to be measured and monitored to ensure learners' knowledge-building. Changing processes consciously and regularly disturbs the complacency that permits the tendency for classroom practices to become routine and less effective. Using many of the Accountable Listening and Talking strategies above makes learning "come alive" and allows classrooms (and PL sessions), anywhere and at any time, to be fun, inspiring, and incredibly vibrant learning places for students, teachers and leaders.

STUDENT VOICES MUST BE HEARD!

Students' voices must be heard more than teachers' voices no matter what the communication vehicle, online or in-class. Teachers in classrooms or leaders at PL sessions must become "evidence-proven" facilitators who, by listening attentively, manage the time for talk, the quality of the talk, and the opportunities for every voice to be heard.

Accountable Listening and Talking must be planned and implemented with the clear understanding that *every voice matters* in every classroom whether it is online or face-to-face teaching and learning. Each voice provides the pulse of the learner/speaker to the teacher; leader/listener. We believe, as many do, that online learning, even using the Accountable Listening and Talking approach, cannot replace the in-person, human interaction that offers all the nonverbal cues to listeners and speakers. When done well, online learning serves as a bridge between life experiences, the "virtual" versus the "real deal" of "being there" as teachers. However, the experience of online learning is that the elements of Accountable Listening and Talk are crucial for the learning or conferencing to be considered "as" or "almost as" effective as classroom or face-to-face learning and dialogue.

LISTENING EXPERIENCES DISCUSSED BY STUDENTS

In January 2024, Sharratt and colleague Amanda Paul, an Ontario secondary teacher, held in-person focus groups of Canadian senior secondary students to hear their reflections on teachers listening to their thinking and talking experiences in school.

Question: What gets in the way of you being an effective listener?

Answer: distractions in the classroom

Answer: when presentations are too long

Answer: when you don't find the topic interesting, so you tune out and you don't listen

Question: What's an example of effective teaching so kids will listen?

Answer:

- ✓ In my bio class, Mr. K, gave us a visual demonstration of where certain organs are in our body by standing up on the chair looking at the projector as well, so there was light illuminating on him. So, I thought that was weird, but it made us remember and listen more.
- ✓ In math, we talked about digits, and then my teacher explained it with a story that made it more interesting and made me listen and remember.

(Continued)

(Continued)

- ✓ We become better listeners when teachers personalize their teaching. I like Think-Alouds, which is when teachers read aloud and make connections to the text for us as they read.

Question: How could teachers be more effective in hearing student views?

Answer: Students spoke about conferencing to provide feedback to students and as a time for assessing students. They stated the most effective conferencing approach with individual students was while the rest of the class was engaged in independent work. It was highlighted that this method allowed for personalized feedback tailored to individual student needs.

Question: How do you know that another person is listening effectively?

Answer: It's only when you can actually do something with what you're listening to that you really are hearing what somebody says.

Question: What classroom strategies did teachers use to help you listen effectively?

Answer: Candy. Your ears opened when there was candy in the room? Yes. They give you candy, so a reward. You can earn candy by listening!

Answer: Getting to really know students and talking to them to have them know you better is something that can create a bond that has a positive outcome of listening in that class. Then teachers know you well enough to say, "These are your strengths." When there's a special relationship, that relationship helps you to listen to what that teacher's saying. Because one of the best ways to get me to listen is if you have a connection to me. Know your students and show them that you care. So that building relationships and having that caring disposition as a teacher is important.

Answer: Some alternative learning strategies, like finding different ways to keep the students engaged, are important to get us to listen. Find out how people like to listen and how they learn differently.

Answer: I appreciate reciprocity in listening. "We haven't heard from these people, does anyone have anything else to add?"

Thanks to their teacher, Ms. Amanda Paul, Grade 11 Business Communication class and Grade 12 Entrepreneurial Studies students engaged actively in our questions and answered honestly, thoughtfully, and impressively. Ms. Paul has summarized the essence of her students' thoughts below:

MAKING PERSONAL CONNECTIONS WITH STUDENTS' THINKING

Student Quote: "I think that is a really key thing for me as a student because anyone can be a teacher. All you have to do is create what you think is material and teach it to the class. But getting to really know your students and talking to them to get them to know you better can create a bond. And the positive outcome could be the bond that leads to listening in class and doing the work."

Teacher's Reflection: This student emphasizes the importance of teachers establishing personal connections with their students. The quote suggests that effective teaching and active listening in class are facilitated when teachers go beyond merely presenting material and strive to understand and connect with their students on a personal level.

ACTIVE LISTENING VS. PASSIVE LISTENING

Student Quote: "It's only when you can actually do something with what you're listening to that you really are hearing what somebody says."

Teacher's Reflection: The focus is on the distinction between simply hearing words and actively engaging with the information being conveyed. Active listening involves processing and applying what is heard, representing a deeper and more involved form of learning than passive listening.

INFLUENCE OF KNOWLEDGE LEVEL ON LISTENING

Student Quote: "If I know a lot more in a certain class, I'm probably not going to listen that much." So, you need your teacher to be smarter than you, is that what you're saying?" "Yeah. Because if I already know what they're saying, why would I listen?"

Teacher's Reflection: This student expresses that their willingness to listen in class is affected by their preexisting knowledge of the subject matter. This perspective implies that when students perceive that they already understand the content, their motivation to listen decreases, highlighting the need for educators to understand and activate prior knowledge, continually challenging students with a differentiated depth of content or query based on that understanding of what the students wants to know more about in order to keep them engaged.

LISTENING TO UNDERSTAND NEEDS AND MAKE DECISIONS

Student Quote: "In the business that I created, I usually just know what people want. If you don't listen to what everyone is saying but buy something that maybe only a couple of people want, you will go broke! Most of the time you actually need to listen to what people say or you buy a lot of what no one wants to buy from you."

Teacher's Reflection: This student in our Venture Class discusses how listening is crucial in understanding the wants and needs of others in the context of buying clothing stock that he could then sell to them. This student realizes listening is particularly important in business and entrepreneurship, where success often hinges on accurately gauging and responding to customer preferences and demands. The reflection of what this student said on knowing the learner could not be more clearly stated.

LISTENING AS A KEY COMMUNICATION SKILL POST-HIGH SCHOOL

Student Quote: "The most important skill you need to have outside high school is communication. A lot of you are not listening. Listening is definitely a skill you will have to learn outside of high school. You're all going to need listening skills as a big part of being a great communicator."

Teacher's Reflection: Here, the emphasis (by an older student who had returned to school) is on the essential role of listening in effective communication, particularly after high school, when [one's] life opportunities will depend on the quality of [one's] listening. This student underscores that listening is an active skill that needs development and is crucial for successful interactions in various life scenarios. Note from LDS: A compelling thought underlying this student's reflections on his past and their common future as graduates, is that he felt comfortable in the culture the teacher had created to permit himself to be vulnerable in expressing his learning, from his "unusual" experience as a mature student.

EFFECTIVE COMMUNICATION AND RELATIONSHIPS

Student Quote: "One of the best ways to get [students] to listen to the teacher is if the teachers connect with their students and show them that they care."

Teacher's Reflection: This student's quote emphasizes the importance of building personal connections and demonstrating care in the context of a teacher-student relationship. It suggests that effective communication and listening in a classroom are significantly enhanced when students feel understood, and, cared for by their teachers.

ADAPTING TO DIFFERENT LEARNING ENVIRONMENTS

Student Quote: "I listen when teachers align with my ideas. If they're talking about what I think is true, let's say, the right way to do something or if they are close to my opinion on something, that's how I listen and engage."

Teacher's Reflection: This student's perspective sheds light on how personal resonance with the content or teaching approach affects their engagement in a learning environment. It highlights that students are more inclined to listen and participate when (a) the material aligns with their own ideas and their depth of understanding of the subject; and when (b) the instructional approach the teacher uses captures students' attention. Taking time to learn about each student's prior learning and knowledge pays off in building relevance, therefore in earning student engagement.

LEARNING FROM NONCLASSROOM SOURCES

Student Quote: "So for me, for example, I learned a lot from my cousins because they're a lot more intelligent than I am. And since I don't have anyone in the house that I can really talk to, unintentionally, whenever I speak to them over the phone or on video games or whatever it may be, I listen and just pick up on a lot of the things that they've spoken about and how they speak and how they put their thoughts out there."

> "'Listening' is more about building active understanding as is demonstrated by the capacity for meaningful application than is passive understanding. We want to enhance student success by building relevant, meaningful, mobilizable application of learning by actively engaging students in relevant learning opportunities."
>
> Ms. Amanda Paul, Secondary School Teacher, Ontario.
>
> Source: In conversation with L. Sharratt, January 21, 2024.

Teacher's Reflection: This quote illuminates the importance of informal learning and the role of listening outside traditional educational settings. This student shares how conversations with family members, particularly cousins, have contributed to his learning and growth, highlighting that valuable knowledge and insights can be gained through informal listening. The quote also restates the extremely powerful notion of knowing as much as possible about the personal background and situation of every student in the class.

The students' thoughts expressed in these group conversations were not surprising; however, they reprised the clarion call for us, as educators, to get busy and listen—and set the parameters for student listening! These senior secondary students summed up their thoughts by saying the following which is a perfect re-telling of the "Five Ear" Model.

So, we listen, we hear what people are saying, we talk about it to understand it, then we take action and apply what we've heard.

The Grade eleven and twelve students offered similar views of listening in their respective focus groups. From each perspective, they emphasized the importance of teachers understanding individual student needs and adapting their teaching strategies accordingly. Similarly, they discussed the significance of teachers building a rapport with their students to create conducive learning environments. Their messages to beginning teachers emphasized the value of building respectful and mutually beneficial relationships between teachers and students to enhance effective listening and learning in their classes. They were clear about the scaffolding that they needed in their classrooms which reflected our model:

I attend, I hear, I understand, I appraise, I activate.

We learn best with and from each other within a deliberately created and carefully nurtured culture of learning and when the mutually inclusive and inseparable twins—Accountable Listening and Accountable Talking—lead the way. In this environment, new knowledge is built, communication skills are improved, and all learners flourish. This is the goal. Students engage in listening and speaking for various purposes in both formal and informal contexts. They develop an awareness of appropriate communication behaviors, learn strategies to comprehend spoken information, and express their thoughts clearly and effectively (Revised Ontario Curriculum, 2023). We now take a Deliberate Pause to apply what we have learned in this chapter.

DELIBERATE PAUSE

To teach the intricacies of nonverbal listening cues, set up a simulation, using the "Three-Step Interview" process:

Person #1: Presenter

Person #2: Listener

Person #3: Observer

Have students in triads assume the roles. The Presenter reads a passage (handed out); the Listener listens and gives positive, nonverbal feedback (debriefed in previous lesson); the observer feeds back what was noticed; the Presenter validates observations (or not) by describing the effect of the Listener's nonverbal cues. Switch roles. The second Listener gives nonverbal, negative cues. Process above is repeated. The third person to play the Listener role gives no response to the reading. The above process is repeated. This process is an opportunity to teach the importance of listening to verbal and nonverbal cues, what that looks like, and what works best to refine students' listening techniques.

A key variation on this exercise adds a verbal interaction component (I understand, I appraise) during which the Listener—after a round of Listening only—is directed to ask the Speaker between one and three questions for clarification. The Questioner can offer cues to the Speaker about their understanding prior to the questioning and as they are listening to the Speaker's—physical responses can show their understanding. The Observer is to note the interaction, watching and listening for the words used and the body messaging (body language). The interaction will produce an observably different interpersonal dynamic. What will the Observer see?

Our Five Ear model sequence of attending, hearing, understanding, appraising, and activating leads to critical thinking (the complex interaction of skills, resources, and "thinking aloud") and propels students, teachers, and leaders to think creatively and reflectively. To facilitate moving toward this goal, all learning experiences in every setting must be scaffolded and differentiated so that learning is progressive, engaging, empowering, and provides a foundation for future learning. This repetitive sequencing must be done across all classes every student takes at every grade level with differentiation for years of learning, of course. The more we listen first, process what we have heard, and talk second in response to what we have heard, the more we learn; and the more we learn, the more we grow and achieve. The next chapter engages us in how we measure listening skills.

COMMITMENT

I commit to:

1. *Listening to and intently hearing students' voices to inform my practice.*
2. *Aiding students to use the Five Ears process in my classes and assisting my teaching staff and leaders in my system to use the same Five Ears process to ensure they communicate thoroughly with each other, learning precisely what each other is saying and intending to mean.*
3. *Understanding the research that points to the power of Accountable Listening and Talking being a pillar of quality teaching in every classroom.*
4. *Understanding how Accountable Listening and Talking Moves must be well-planned and thoughtfully executed.*
5. *Working alongside others to co-plan, co-teach, co-debrief, and co-reflect to embed Accountable Listening and Talking in our Unit and Lesson Plans.*

CHAPTER 7

MEASURING LISTENING SKILLS

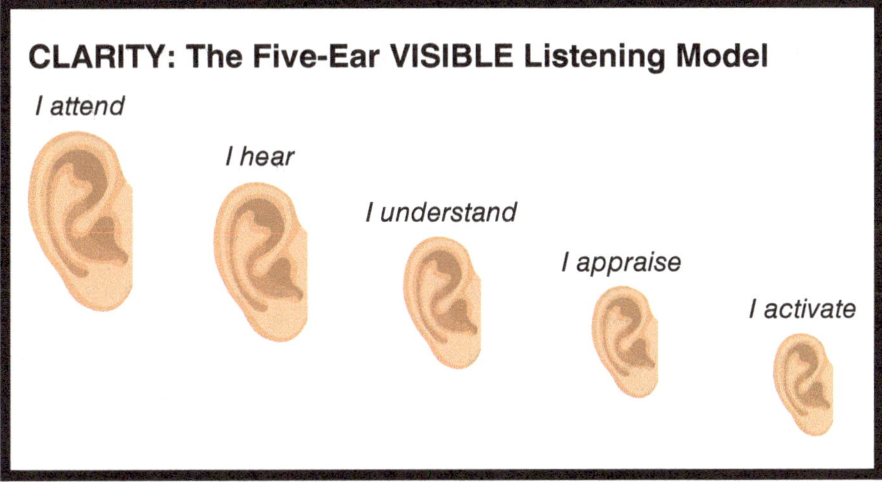

We continue to understand the art and craft of "listening" and clarify its meaning throughout this text. Recently, Kluger and Mizrahi (2023) asked ChatGPT 3: "The noun 'listening' is often preceded by an adjective, such as in active listening, empathic listening, and deep listening. What are the 15 most common adjectives of listening?" ChatGPT answered: attentive, focused, engaged, nonjudgmental, open-minded, empathetic, reflective, active, deep, critical, mindful, selective, conscious, and effective." (ChatGPT could only count to fourteen!). From their analysis of adjectives to describe listening, they proposed that listening "is the degree to which a person devotes themselves to co-explore the other with and for the other (p. 4)." This comes back to the notion we explored earlier about the dignity and respect that can accrue from listening: "the state of listening is an interpersonal state co-created by the devotion of both speaker and listener to be present together." (p. 7). And we ask, "how do we measure it"?

The broad scope of measurement of listening in research and writing covers listening related to ear issues (phases of deafness), listening to sounds as a precursor to reading, listening in counseling, listening in second language classes, and, too rarely, the skills of listening by teachers and students. What we want to know from the measurement is "Do they attend, hear, understand, appraise and can they act on what was heard, or was meant to be heard (activate)?" Answering this question is the focus of our book and is the main purpose of this chapter (see also Buck, 2001; Rost, 2020).

We explore the current measures of listening primarily to ascertain the key dimensions that various scholars have considered important. Not all lack critique, but the more *important consideration for this book is the identification of the major dimensions of listening* across these tests.

CURRENT LISTENING ASSESSMENTS

Fontana et al. (2015) located fifty-three listening competency scales. They start by seeing two major conceptions of listening—as a process (how we process information) and as a product (the effectiveness of receiving the message). They then identified the traits that appear in a majority of the scales (the following were in at least twenty-seven of the fifty-three scales):

- Responds: Listener responds or gives feedback
- Questions: Listener asks questions
- Nonverbal: Listener uses nonverbal communication
- Understands: General understanding

Other common dimensions include attention, non-verbal listening, understanding feelings or emotions, non-interruption skills, showing interest, paraphrasing the speaker, and clearly responding. Surprisingly, there were fewer scale dimensions about understanding the speaker's perspective, showing comfort while listening, and freedom from distractions when another is talking. Fontana et al. (2015) were surprised at how dissimilar the scales were in measuring the various dimensions, suggesting that researchers have different ideas as to what constitutes competent listening. The most common listening attributes include responding or giving feedback, asking questions, and using nonverbal communication.

Oscar and Luella Buros pioneered the *Mental Measurements Yearbook*. First published in 1939, this has become the bible of measurement and includes reviews of the most used measures. Now, our friend and colleague Kurt Geisinger leads it, and it remains the most credible and valuable resource of published tests in English. The latest edition lists sixteen listening measures (excluding tests specific to foreign languages or adults).

1. The *Listening Skills Inventory* (2011) aims to measure how attentive students are to a speaker and the degree of active participation in the **listening** process. It is a self-administered online assessment, measuring two major factors and seven subscales: (1) Physical Attentiveness—External Distractions, Conversation Flow, Speaker to Listener Transition, Body Language; and (2) Mental Attentiveness—Internal Distractions, Attention Span, Hearing a Person Out. The reviewers were highly critical of the lack of information about the development of this measure but did note it had a large standardization sample of 23,220 participants, and at best, recommended it as a screening measure.

2. The *Test of Academic Achievement Skills—Reading, Arithmetic, Spelling, and Listening Comprehension* is for four to twelve-year-old children. The Listening Comprehension subtests requires the examiner to read a short passage to the student and orally ask five to six questions about the passage. This is important to ensure the scores are not biased by students' reading skills so the passages are read to the students, but the reviewers find the "questions are limited," and some of the passages "provide a poor match to the backgrounds of many school-age children" (one is about visiting a family friend, the senator—a highly context specific example and will not be readily understood by all students).

3. The *Listening Skills Test* (Lloyd et al., 2001) is for three to seven-year-olds and consists of forty-five items assessing children's ability to make decisions about verbal information as "they hear it." There are four subtests: Referent Identification (the ability to detect ambiguity in messages), Message Appraisal (the ability to judge statements as true or false), Comprehension of Directions (the ability to follow an extended set of instructions), and Verbal Message Evaluation (the ability to evaluate the content of verbal statements without context cues) as well as producing an overall score. It is claimed that the scores can be used to evaluate the students' skills in accommodating the "business of the classroom." That is, can they make appropriate decisions about linguistic messages directly impacting on their school success? Some of the score estimates of reliability are far below acceptable levels (e.g., Verbal Message ranges from .07 – .55), which make them not much better than random numbers. The reviewers note that the usefulness is limited, some instructions are confusing and difficult to use with young children, the reliability is far too low, and the test seems "not quite finished."

4. The *Oral and Written Language Scales* (Brunsman & Person, 2014) has 130 listening comprehension items measuring listening to and comprehending spoken language. Applicable for three to twenty-one-year-old students, each item is multiple choice, and the respondent is requested to point to a response from the pictures/words. The norms are based on 2,123 students, and there are three listening scores: (1) Lexical/Semantic items that measure the range of linguistic structures, (2) Syntactic items that require comprehension of noun and verb modulators, and (3) Supralinguistic items that comprise tasks requiring language analysis on a level higher than decoding literal lexical or syntactic structures. The reviewers considered the test could be used to identify those with listening impairments and were impressed with the discussion of intervention principles and case examples.

5. *The Classroom Communication Skills Inventory* (Psychological Corporation, 1993) is a checklist of fifty-two **listening** and speaking skills and behaviors designed for use by a classroom teacher evaluating the students' active listening and participation in classrooms activities. Based on a sample of about five thousand students, the reviewers were concerned with the

subjectivity of scoring, limited validity evidence, and were quite negative about the measurement properties.

6. *The Progressive Achievement Tests of Listening Comprehension* (Reid et al., 2015) aims to assist teachers in determining levels of development their students attain in the basic listening comprehension skills. There are eleven levels, from very limited ability to a very advanced degree of competency in listening comprehension. Norms are based on one thousand students.
7. *The CAT/5 Listening and Speaking Checklist* (Psychological Corporation, 1993) claims to be a checklist but is a series of scales that ask for ratings from one (minimal or rudimentary ability) to three (maximal ability or mastery). The teacher asks students a series of questions to determine whether he or she has correctly comprehended orally presented material. The reviewers could find little to no validity information, the ratings scales are ill defined, and there is no way to gain an overall index of listening proficiency, thus leading them to not recommend its use in classrooms.
8. *LOTE Reading and Listening Tests* for high school students is a short twelve minutes (Zammit, 1991). Students listen to a tape recording of a speaker and then are asked to choose an appropriate response to what they have heard. The test has very low reliability estimates, and the reviewers are cautious about recommending its use.
9. *The Listening Inventory* (Geffner & Ross-Swain, 2006), for students aged four to seventeen, is a screening test to detect auditory processing disorders. It has six subtests: Linguistic Organization, Decoding and Language Mechanics, Attention and Organization, Sensory-Motor Skills, Social and Behavioral Skills, and Auditory Processes. It consists of 103 statements and teachers and/or parents' rating on a 0-5 scale as to the frequency of the behavior. Some items are seen as confusing (ask about the absence of a behavior, or do not tap discrete behaviors). The reviewers welcomed the breadth of content and ease of scoring, but the insufficiency of measurement evidence led them not to recommend the measure for screening.
10. *Word Meaning Through Listening* for years three through eleven, grades three through eleven (Brimer, 2002). Students have sixty items to measure "the understanding of spoken English words

through the recognition of pictures that represent their meaning" (p. 12). The teacher reads a word and then the student chooses which one best represents the word from two pictures. The reviewers had negative comments about the lack of information about the validity claims, the complicated scoring scheme, the conversion to practice ranks and an IQ-like score, and it seems more a vocabulary than a listening measure.

11. *The Listening Comprehension Test Series* (Hagues et al., 1999) is for four to fourteen-year-olds and includes four listening selections followed by multiple choice or true-false items. Passages include short- and medium-length expository, opinion, and narrative texts; multiple-speaker interactions; poems; scenarios; first- and third-person accounts; and assorted classroom-type events. The reviewers noted little discussion of test validity and seemed bemused by the British accents and how that could detract from the performance of North American students.

12. *Learning Through Listening* (Wilkinson et al., 1976) is for thirteen to eighteen-year-old students, and is designed to measure the ability to follow and understand a piece of informal exposition capturing the following measures: contextual constraints, such as the ability to infer missing parts of a conversation from what is actually heard; phonology, or the ability to understand differences in meaning brought about by different emphases; register, which is the ability to detect changes in the appropriateness of the spoken language used; and relationship, the ability to detect the kinds of relationships existing between people from the language they employ. Listening tasks include telephone conversations, reflections on a dream, radio announcements, street conversations, lectures, and conversations among interviewers of candidates for a teaching position. Students then respond to a series of multiple-choice items. The reviewers were bemused by the British sayings and noted the lack of psychometric detail and almost no interpretation of the limited statistical information provided.

13. *The Jones-Mohr Listening Test* (J. E. Jones & Mohr, 1976) measures listening accuracy with a particular emphasis on emotional intentions. This test was developed "to facilitate and evaluate skill-building using emotionally laden statements." Sentences are read to convey various emotions and students are asked to

select from four options that best respect the speaker's intended meaning. They provide no psychometric evidence for the use of scores from this test. As the reviewer commented: "The test is confounded by a number of factors and seriously flawed by the lack of any reliability and validity data."

14. *The Listening Comprehension Test* (Upshur et al., 1972) requires students to listen to sentence-length statements and choose the best of three responses. The reviewers note that the validity arguments are weak, and too much attention is paid to grammatical structures that impede the test, which is a measure of listening.

15. *The Listening Comprehension Test—Adolescent* (Bowers et al., 2009) is a checklist of listening and speaking skills and behaviors aiming to make inferences about a student's abilities to be an active listener and participant in normal classroom instructional settings, to identify areas of strengths and weaknesses in these classroom communication skills, and to suggest underlying reasons for identified weaknesses. Items include "The student learns vocabulary taught in class lessons and uses the words appropriately in class assignments," "The student converses with the teacher in one-on-one situations," "The student talks neither too much nor too little in class," "The student has an adequate vocabulary size," and "The student's voice is appropriate for age and gender." What is appropriate or adequate seems subjective, there is limited validity evidence, and there is a lack of scoring guides. However, the measure provides a valuable list of skills and abilities related to listening and communicating in the classroom.

16. *TAPS-4: A Language Processing Skills Assessment* (Martin et al., 2018) includes a measure of listening comprehension aimed at five to twenty-one-year-olds. The Listening Comprehension subtests assess processing of oral directions, auditory comprehension for passages of varying levels of complexity, and auditory comprehension when challenged with background noise. Based on 2,023 students, the estimates of reliability seem acceptable, the items load where expected in factor models. The test was reviewed as worthwhile for students who are suspected of having difficulties with language processing and comprehension that may not have been identified with other measures of

receptive and expressive language, and in determining specific areas of weakness in language processing (i.e., phonological vs. memory vs. comprehension).

17. *The Watson–Barker Listening Test* (Watson et al., 1991) evaluates five listening competencies: evaluating message content, understanding meaning in conversations, understanding and remembering information in lectures, evaluating emotional meanings in messages, and following instructions and directions. Students watch a video of dialogue and monologues and answer forty items that are scored correct or not. Bodie et al. (2011) failed to support the four expected dimensions and expressed caution about using the scores from this measure.

18. *The Dynamic Assessment Test of Listening Comprehension*, (Brandao et al., 2014) developed for four to six-year-olds, includes twenty passages. Students are asked forty questions, and first, given a chance to answer without prompts followed by opportunities to answer when prompted: first by repetition of the full text excerpt; then by repetition of the portion of the text that contains the information required to produce a correct response; and finally, by presentation of the item using a multiple-choice format. A maximum score of 4 is attributed to the correct response without the use or prompts, three points after the first prompt to 0 when the multiple-choice option is incorrect. Brandao et al. (2014) found the test had acceptable levels of reliability, and there was one dominant listening factor, but it was combined with reading text comprehension—so the total test score measured a combination of listening and comprehension.

Across these many measures, there seem to be five major dimensions of listening.

1. Physical attentiveness includes factors such as listening to minimize external distractions, maintaining conversation flow, speaker-to-listener transition, and mental attentiveness.
2. Internal factors such as attention span and hearing a person out.
3. Comprehension of spoken language includes understanding meaning in conversations, understanding and remembering

information in passages or lectures, evaluating emotional meanings in messages, and considering cultural factors (e.g., accents).

4. Critical Listening Skills such as evaluating message content, following instructions and directions, making decisions about verbal information as heard, judging statements as true or false, and evaluating the content of verbal statements without context cues.

5. Language processing skills, including phonological, memory, and comprehension aspects.

Berninger and Abbott (2010) also asked about the common factors across listening comprehension, oral expression, reading comprehension, and written expression (that is, language by ear, mouth, eye, and hand). They administered tests of these to grades one, three, five, and seven students, including the Weschler Listening Comprehension test that assesses two dimensions: Receptive Vocabulary where students point to one of four pictures that portrayed the meaning of a word pronounced by the examiner; and Expressive Vocabulary where students generate one word that matched a verbal description of a concept provided by the examiner. They found that a multiple-factor model provided a better statistical fit than a one factor model. The only predictor of listening comprehension was prior reading comprehension and they argued that listening and reading comprehension jointly supported the other.

The major themes across these eighteen measures include the following:

- Listening accuracy, evaluation of message content, including detecting ambiguity in message, following instructions and directions, and evaluating the content of verbal statements without context cues.

- Conversation flow, including understanding meaning in conversations, the ability to infer missing parts of a conversation from what is actually heard, understanding differences in meaning brought about by different emphases, the ability to detect changes in the appropriateness of the spoken language used, speaker-to-listening transition, hearing a person out, and avoiding distractions.

- Detecting emotional intentions.

These three major themes need to be assessed across many varied settings.

Gilson et al. (2024) developed the Teacher Listening Orientation Questionnaire (TLOQ) to measure teachers' perceptions of listening. They begin by noting the dominance of monological discourse in classrooms, especially the well-known and well researched IRE model—teacher **I**nitiation usually via a question (I), followed by a student **R**esponse (R), and ending with a teacher **E**valuation of the accuracy of the student's response (E). Or the variant IRF, where the teacher instead of commenting on the accuracy or not of the student response incudes a **F**ollow-up (F) moving to the next question. Both these patterns require teacher listening skills, but it seems only minimal teacher listening skills.

If, however, there is more dialogic discourse, then the listening skills of both teachers and students become more critical. Gilson et al. show that such discourse can lead to much richer interactions, including more opportunities "for (a) extended teacher follow-ups, (b) student participation, (c) enhanced cognitive engagement, (d) interactive exchanges about different ideas, (e) higher-level and open-ended questions, and (f) shared responsibility in co-constructing knowledge between and among the students and teacher" (p 3). These listening skills go to the heart of the International Listening Association's (International Listening Association, 1995) claim which states that listening is "the process of receiving (I attend), constructing meaning from (I hear, and I understand), and responding to spoken and/or non-verbal messages" (I appraise, and I activate) (p. 4). There is active more than passive listening; there is reciprocal and active meaning making; there is (are) response(s); and often there is deeper reconceptualization by teachers and students about the focus of the dialogue.

Gilson et al. used 536 teachers mainly from America and across all grade levels. The thirty-two-item TLOQ was developed to measure six major factors:

1. **Evaluative Listening Orientation.** The teacher listens primarily for predetermined responses to questions during a discussion (e.g., expected comments, answers, keywords, phrases).
2. **Interpretive Listening Orientation.** The teacher listens primarily for student understanding.
3. **Participatory Student-Oriented Listening.** The teacher listens primarily as an active participant in an authentic conversation with students.

4. **Facilitative Student-Oriented Listening.** The teacher listens primarily to facilitate authentic student-to-student discussions.

5. **Participatory/Facilitative Student-Oriented Listening.** The teacher's listening is a combination of the defining characteristics of participatory and facilitative.

6. **Listening for Student Talk.** The teacher listens primarily to sustain and encourage in-depth student talk during a discussion.

But the results of their factor analyses reduced this from six to three clearer factors: Evaluative, Interpretive, and Participatory/Facilitative Student Orientation. This led the authors to claim that their measures relate to listening as a reciprocal, active, and interpersonal process of meaning-making and responding. Those five items, with highest factor loadings on their respective factor, include the following success criteria:

Evaluative Listening

1. I can listen to point out the accuracy of students' answers.
2. I can listen to know if students can recall specific information.
3. I can listen for particular key words in students' responses.
4. I can listen for opportunities to praise accurate answers.
5. I can listen for correct information in students' comments.

Interpretive Listening

6. I can listen to figure out how students are making sense of the lesson.
7. I can listen to formulate questions that will help students expand on their responses.
8. I can listen to clarify my interpretation of students' answers.
9. I can listen to students' explanations that help me understand how I can support students' learning
10. I can listen to determine how to guide students in learning the lesson objectives.

(Continued)

(Continued)

Participatory/Facilitative Student-Oriented Listening

11. I can listen for chances to talk about students' unique insights about the topic.
12. I can listen so students will take the lead in sharing a variety of opinions with one another.
13. I can listen so students will direct a conversation about opposing perspectives related to the topic of discussion.
14. I can listen so students take primary ownership of the discussion.
15. I can listen to students' points-of-view even if I do not agree.

While we excluded measures of listening specific to languages in this book, the field of second language learning has a more systematic history of ideas about listening (although it tends to be focused more on post-high school) measurement of listening. Ji et al. (2022) completed a systematic review and argued that listening anxiety includes tenseness, irritation, frustration, apprehension, nervousness, and uneasiness, and such anxiety can lead to apprehension and negative self-evaluations. Across the thirty-three measures they located, most measured worry and emotionality, and they tended to use one of three approaches focusing on the psychological, the social, or the situation specific.

From the listing above of detailed references to research about listening it is unclear how any assessments or measures have developed definitions of listening that can be taught or learned. Working from the research, including the second language post-secondary research, it may be possible to simplistically summarize the keys to "listening," which can be learned and taught within a dialogue as the following:

- listening (hearing) to understand what is being said;
- asking oneself what one is hearing means within one's own world of understanding and context;

- asking the speaker clarification questions based on what has been heard and what one already understands;
- hearing the secondary or responsive statement from the speaker; and
- agreeing on the meaning.

The Revised Ontario Language Curriculum (2023, pp. 95–140) Canada is very clear about the central place of Listening in the Curriculum. This curriculum evaluates Listening Skills in the following contexts:

CLEAR EXPECTATIONS FOR TEACHING AND MEASURING LISTENING SKILLS

1. Purpose: Identify purposes for listening in a variety of situations, formal and informal, and set personal goals for listening, initially with support and direction (e.g., to acquire information from a presentation by a guest speaker; to exchange ideas in a small-group discussion; to enjoy and understand poetry).
2. Active Listening Strategies: Demonstrate an understanding of appropriate listening behavior by using active listening strategies in a variety of situations (e.g., demonstrate understanding of when to speak, when to listen, and how much to say; restate what the speaker has said and connect it to their own ideas; express personal interest in what has been said by asking related questions: I like what ________ said about ________).

   Teacher prompt: "When First Nations peoples use a talking stick, a person speaks only when holding the talking stick, while the rest of the group listens. Today we are going to speak and listen in a similar way."
3. **Comprehension Strategies:** Identify several listening comprehension strategies and use them before, during, and after listening in order to understand and clarify the meaning of oral texts (e.g., listen for key words and phrases that signal important ideas; retell an oral text to a partner after a presentation; ask appropriate questions in order to make predictions about an oral text).

4. **Demonstrating Understanding:** Demonstrate an understanding of the information and ideas in oral texts by retelling the story or restating the information, including the main idea and several interesting details (e.g., restate a partner's reflections after a think-pair-share activity; identify the important ideas in a group presentation; carry on a sustained conversation on a topic).

5. **Making Inferences/Interpreting Texts:** Use stated and implied information and ideas in oral texts to make simple inferences and reasonable predictions and support the inferences with evidence from the text.

   Teacher prompt: "You predicted ________. What clues from the oral text did you use to figure that out?"

   OVERALL EXPECTATIONS By the end of grade two, students will: 1. listen in order to understand and respond appropriately in a variety of situations for a variety of purposes; 2. use speaking skills and strategies appropriately to communicate with different audiences for a variety of purposes; 3. reflect on and identify their strengths as listeners and speakers, areas for improvement, and the strategies they found most helpful in oral communication situations.

   SPECIFIC EXPECTATIONS * Talking sticks were initially used by some First Nations peoples to ensure impartial and fair council meetings, but their use is becoming popular again in talking and sentencing circles. A person speaks only when holding the talking stick, while the rest of the group listens silently.

6. **Oral Communication:** Extend understanding of oral texts by connecting the ideas in them to their own knowledge and experience; to other familiar texts, including print and visual texts; and to the world around them (e.g., talk about their own ideas and experiences related to the topic before listening; connect ideas from oral presentations to related school and community events and/or to other texts with similar topics or themes, including multicultural texts or texts in their own first language).

7. **Analysing Texts:** Identify words or phrases that indicate whether an oral text is fact or opinion, initially with support and

direction (e.g., phrases such as I think . . . I feel . . . I wonder . . . indicate an opinion rather than strictly factual information).

8. **Point of View:** Identify, initially with support and direction, who is speaking in an oral text and demonstrate an understanding that the speaker has his or her own point of view (e.g., people, events, and details are viewed differently by different people).

   Teacher prompts: "Does who is talking affect how the information is presented or how the story is told?" "How do you know the speaker's feelings about the topic? How does that affect you as a listener?" "How might the text change if [character X] were speaking instead?"

9. **Presentation Strategies:** Identify some of the presentation strategies used in oral texts and explain how they influence the audience (e.g., the use of facial expressions helps the listener understand what is being said).

   Teacher prompts: "How does looking at the expression on a speaker's face help you to understand what is being said?" "Does the look on the speaker's face somehow change the meaning of the actual words being spoken?"

10. **Active Listening Strategies:** Demonstrate an understanding of appropriate listening behavior by adapting active listening strategies to suit a range of situations, including working in groups (e.g., asking questions to clarify understanding before responding; affirming and building on the ideas of others; summarizing and responding constructively to ideas expressed by others; using brief vocal prompts to signal agreement or interest during conversations: Yes; Say that again, please; Tell me more).

11. **Comprehension Strategies:** Identify a variety of listening comprehension strategies and use them appropriately before, during, and after listening in order to understand and clarify the meaning of oral texts (e.g., ask questions about facts, inferences, and value judgements to focus and clarify understanding of the themes in an oral text; summarize and synthesize ideas to deepen understanding of an oral text; use self-questioning and predict questions that might be asked to monitor understanding while listening).

12. **Metacognition Strategies:** Identify, in conversation with the teacher and peers, what strategies they found most helpful before, during, and after listening and speaking and what steps they can take to improve their oral communication skills.

Teacher prompts: "What strategies do you use to help you understand and follow a discussion among several people?" "What strategies do you use to recall important information after listening?" "What factors do you consider when deciding whether to use an informal or a formal approach when speaking?"

Teacher prompts: "What listening strategies help you to contribute effectively in a group discussion?" "What questions do you ask yourself to check whether you are understanding what is being said?" "Can you identify the most effective elements in your oral presentation? How do you know they were effective?" "What would you do differently next time?"

> I believe as educators, we need to teach our students what it means to listen, that is, engage in "active listening." They need to know how to get their bodies still, be ready to take in the information, how to focus their eyes on the speaker, and how to note the many visual cues provided by the speaker. We need to practice with our students. We need to give them opportunities to engage in "active listening," to have them respond and engage in conversations with others to further their understanding of what they have heard.
>
> Lorie Sorger-Needham, Primary Teacher, Ontario, Canada.

QUESTIONS TO PROMPT STUDENTS' SELF-ASSESSMENT OF THEIR LISTENING SKILLS

Teaching students to be self-assessors is a helpful way to make them aware of how they learn to listen. The following are some examples of questions to ensure metacognition:

- "What questions can you ask yourself while listening to be sure that you understand what you hear?"
- "What can you do after listening to check that you have understood?"

- "How do you get ready to speak?"
- "While you are speaking, how do you check whether you are keeping the attention of your audience?
- "How does listening make you a better speaker?"
- "How does viewing texts help you when you are listening?"
- "How does your "author's notebook" help you as a writer?"
- "How does listening to stories help you when you are writing?"
- "How might listening to movies or television programs you watch help you as a listener and writer?"
- "What questions do you ask yourself after listening to check that you have understood?"
- "How do you check to ensure the audience understands what you are saying?"
- "How does speaking make you a better listener?"
- "How does seeing a television program on a topic help you when you are discussing that topic in class?"
- "Does learning new words from your reading help you when you are listening to oral texts?"
- "What strategies do you use to monitor your listening to ensure you understand the speaker?"
- "If, after listening, you think you don't understand, what steps do you take to clear up your confusion?"
- "How do you identify what you do well as a speaker and what you would like to improve upon?"
- "How can viewing media texts help you as a listener or speaker?"
- "What strategies do you use to monitor your listening to ensure you understand the speaker?"
- "If, after listening, you think you don't understand, what steps do you take to clear up your confusion?"
- "How do you identify what you do well as a speaker and what you would like to improve upon?"

- "How can viewing media texts help you as a listener or speaker?"
- "How does it help you to listen to someone else read your writing?"
- "What messages did you get from the speaker's tone of voice/ body language/facial expressions?"
- "How does paying attention to a speaker's body language help you interpret what is being said?"
- "What do you try to find out before listening to an oral text?"
- "How can a partner help you clarify your ideas after listening to an oral text?"
- "How do you think listening to oral texts has helped you become a better writer?"

We now consider a Deliberate Pause to investigate further a practical way for teachers to measure students' ability to listen and co-construct Listening Success Criteria.

DELIBERATE PAUSE

We are reflecting on the evaluation of the five stages of listening that we have learned:

1. Attending
2. Hearing
3. Understanding
4. Appraising
5. Activating

See the QR Code in the graphic for Reading Passage about Listening by John Hattie and Lyn Sharratt. Then ask students the 5 Questions. Evaluate their answers together. Co-Construct Success Criteria with students for attentive listening skills.

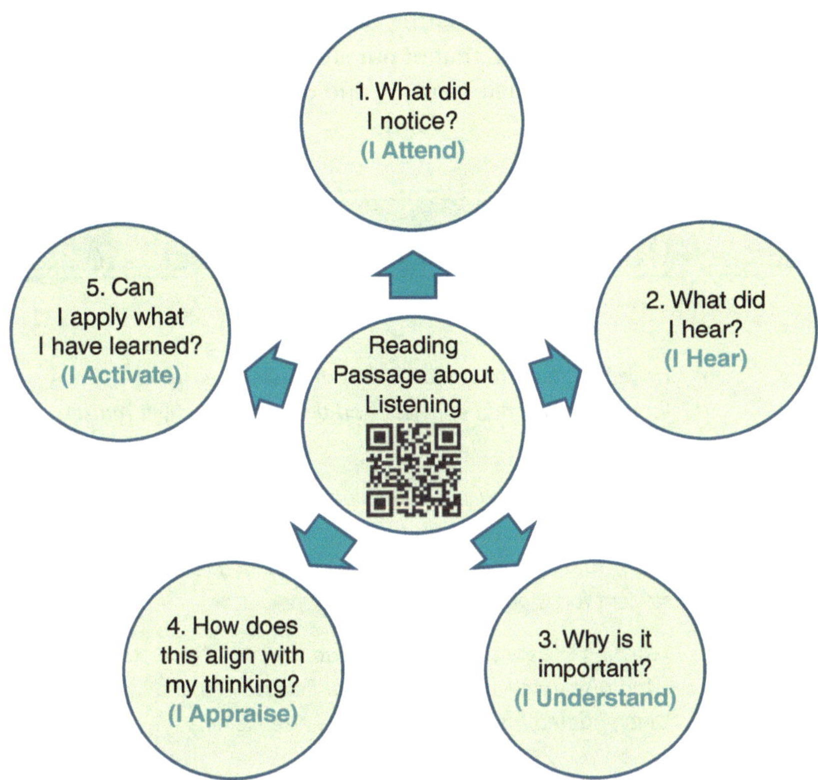

There is power in being heard and in having someone understand one's perspective even if they don't agree with it. Actively listening to understand will lead to stronger and more acceptable conclusions or solutions for the speaker and the listener rather than simply listening could generate. That's where the power lies for collaborative entities like classrooms, school systems or societies. As educators, we know that listening for understanding is an important skill to be taught and modeled so that students learn to become critical thinkers. The notion of dialogic instruction where a teacher presents *and* probes for understanding and *responds* to queries is a clear example of modeling active listening for understanding. We know from the research that students learn best through an attentive listening process as exemplified by the Gradual Release/Acceptance of Responsibility that progresses from Attending, Hearing, Understanding, Appraising to Activating new knowledge in classrooms. Evaluating our ability to continually assess effective listening—our own, that of our students and our colleagues—is crucially important to their learning and our leadership.

COMMITMENT

I commit to:

1. *Understanding the research that discusses measuring listening skills and behaviors and determining why it matters to me in my context.*
2. *Implementing a purposeful dialogic approach in my teaching where I will actively listen to and intently hear my students' voices to make my practice more precise and to increase student focus and comprehension levels.*
3. *Teaching the continuum of I Attend, I Hear, I Understand, I Appraise, I Activate as a Gradual Release Model of Differentiated Instruction—not one size fits all.*

We now turn our attention to **how** Listening Skills can be woven throughout the school improvement approach to ensure *all* students are growing and achieving.

CHAPTER 8

LISTENING ENHANCES THE SCHOOL IMPROVEMENT WORK

A Case Study

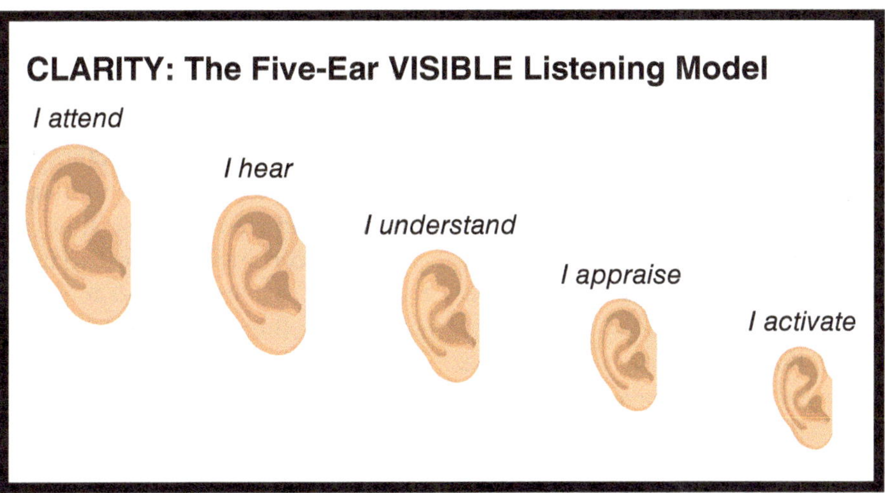

In 2023, Melissa Kable, assistant principal of curriculum and instruction at Killarney Vale Primary School (KVPS), a 470-student school on the Central Coast of New South Wales (NSW), Australia, emailed Sharratt with a story of growth and achievement. "I want to share our school's story of improvement that is the result of our reading and implementing *CLARITY*. I want you to know the impact your book is having in our school (Sharratt, 2019)." In this case study, Kable has woven together the critical importance of **listening** to each other's thinking and the elements of CLARITY in moving the school achievement levels forward on behalf of all students.

THE STARTING POINT

Acknowledging and concerned that its school performance could be improved, the KVPS leadership team initiated a staff-wide book-study and developed follow-up Professional Learning (PL) based on the text *CLARITY: What Matters Most in Learning, Teaching, and Leading* (2019).

Staff formally reviewed their data together. The NAPLAN results (a National Standards-based Assessment in Australia) indicated the need to focus on numeracy, a focus supported by very low school performance scores on the NSW Common Grade Assessment (Essential Assessment – assessment and curriculum tool). On the pretest, targets were not met in grades kindergarten to six, as shown in Figure 8.1. (Midyear assessment in June and the final post-year assessment are held in November.)

A WORK IN PROGRESS

Kable explained, "We began our new PL at the beginning of 2022, the first PL since March 2020 due to COVID restrictions and staff shortages. Jeanette Dillon, the principal at the time, had read *CLARITY* after colleagues suggested the book to her." Kable continued, "The Executive team led the book study using *CLARITY*, unpacking chapters to gain a deep knowledge and better understanding of the research and practices that work in improving schools. The team established a focus represented by the Watermark 'Consistency' (*CLARITY*, Chapter 1), as this underpinned everything we were trying to do, with the school improvement plan across all processes in the school." At this point in Kable's narrative, "I reacted," said Sharratt. "*My attentive listening ears* were switched on with the sole intent to *understand* precisely the steps that Kable and the staff had taken."

Figure 8.1 2021 Number and Algebra Results Are "In the Red"

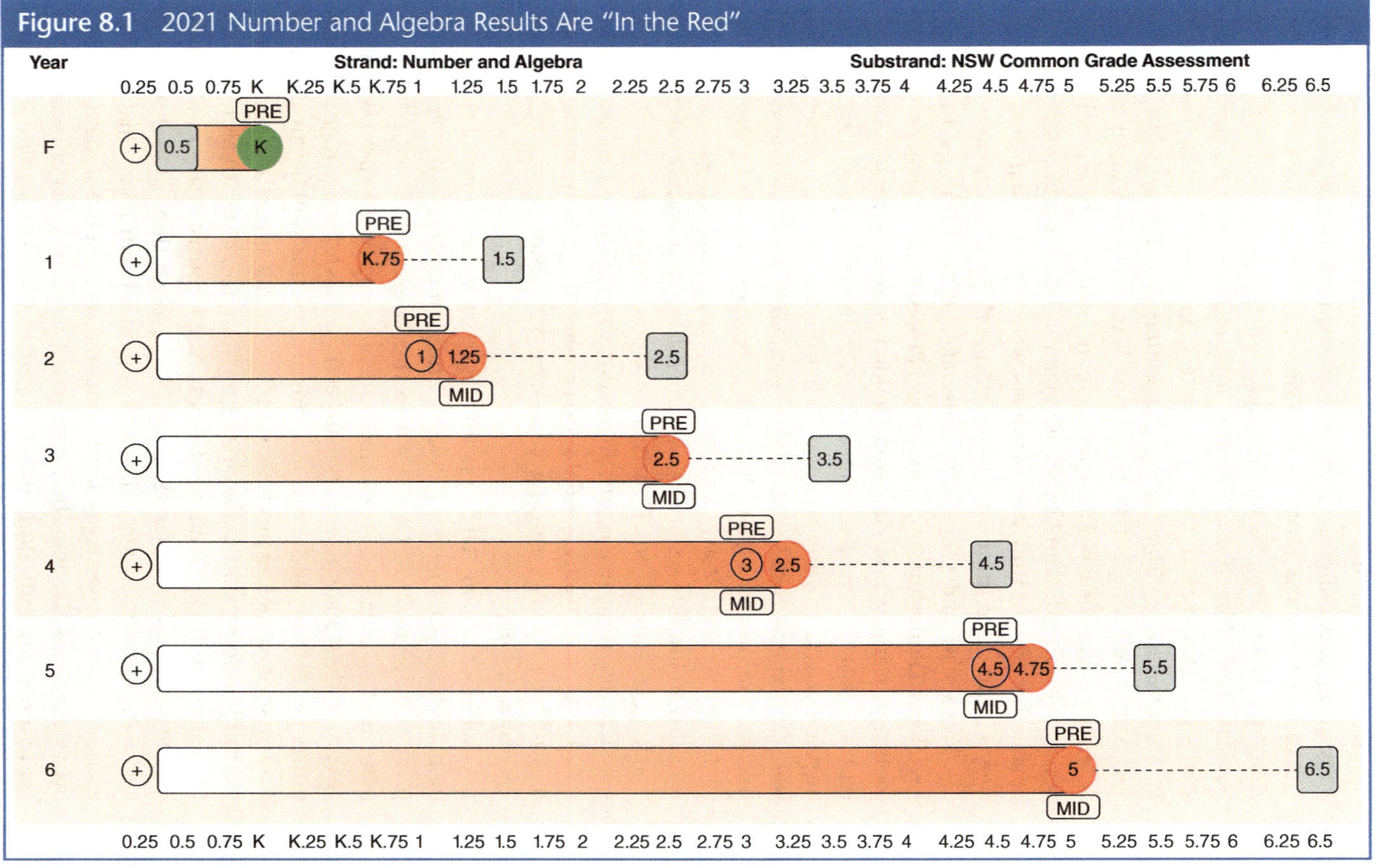

Source: Created by Melissa Kable. Used with permission.

To enable ongoing assessment of the new learning, Kable created a staff and leadership team self-assessment tool for the 14 Parameters, cross-referencing the NSW School Excellence Framework's three review elements: Delivering, Sustaining and Growing, and Excelling. The initial data from March 2022 formed a baseline for the PL showing the staff were: *Delivering* in eight Parameters, *Sustaining* and *Growing* in six Parameters, and *Excelling* in no Parameters (see Figure 8.2). This process demanded complete suspension of leadership's personal biases and acceptance that others knew more about elements of the school processes than they did, and becoming open to hearing and understanding what other leaders and staff members were saying, what they thought they should do to improve the situation as defined by the data.

KVPS staff had previously undertaken other PL using the School Excellence Framework and High Impact Professional Learning assessment tools and found those elements blended well with the CLARITY content. Kable said, "We determined that we needed to pull these together beginning with the end in mind. What did we want to achieve? What were our expectations? What pedagogical changes did we need to make to ensure improved student learning outcomes? Numeracy groups were trialed where staff slowly chipped away at improving teacher practice resulting in improved student outcomes. High Expectations and Explicit Teaching became a focus. Consistency of practice became the norm. Staff felt their learning needs and suggestions were listened to and understood. Improved numeracy data was celebrated regularly, and staff could see their decisions regarding consistent "precision-in-practice" "were making a difference."

Kable said, "Our starting point was to focus on knowing the FACES of all learners (Parameter #1)." Kable and staff created Data Walls in the private Staff Learning Centre where they were out of sight from students and parents. Kable described the outcome of the first Data Walls, "Every student's FACE was known—achievers who were: high, low and under-performing. Rich conversations at the Data Wall began about the students whose lack of progress was immediately apparent. Teachers and learning support staff collaborated on how to guide student learning (Parameter #6). Data conversations focused consistently on improved student outcomes rather than defensive posturing. Staff learned to authentically exhibit reciprocal listening as all staff had valuable information about the needs of many students—not just the students in their own classrooms. Teachers became excited about meetings in which they could move students along the Data Wall to witness how *their* improved

Figure 8.2 14 Parameters Self-Assessment Tool Referencing the NSW School Excellence Framework

14 Parameters Self-assessment	Term 1 Week 9	MASTER		
Parameter		**Delivering**	**Sustaining & Growing**	**Excelling**
1.	**Shared Beliefs and Understanding**			
1. All students can achieve high standards given the right time and the right support. 2. All teachers can teach to high standards given time and the right assistance. 3. High expectations and early and ongoing intervention are essential. 4. All leaders, teachers, and students can articulate what they do and why they lead, teach and learn the way they do.				
2.	**Embedded Knowledgeable Others**			
• These **Knowledgeable Others** are instructional coaches who have time purposefully scheduled during the school day to work alongside classroom teachers, supporting focused work on assessment that informs instruction. • **Knowledgeable Others** must have strong interpersonal skills to build relational trust while collaborating with teachers.				
3.	**Quality Assessment Informs Instruction**			
• Evidence-proven, high-impact practices, like using ongoing assessment data that differentiate instruction, are embedded in the planning for daily, specific subject classes where every lesson features a literacy skill and teachers embed **assessment for and as learning** practices to inform the next steps for instruction. • **Gradual Release and Acceptance of Responsibility** (GRR) model to ensure precision in practice.				

(Continued)

(Continued)

Parameter	Delivering	Sustaining & Growing	Excelling
4. **Principal as Lead Learner**			
Instructional leaders: • Put FACES on the data and take action to make a difference for all students. • Acquire a deep understanding of effective classroom practices by participating in ongoing professional Collaborative Inquiry about high-impact practices. • Take part, with their leadership teams, in system learning sessions and plan how they will replicate the learning back in their schools. • Conduct Learning Walks and Talks daily in classrooms.			
5. **Early and Ongoing Interventions**			
• Individual student need is determined by the ongoing scrutiny of a variety of assessment data. • A structured, collaboratively planned approach by all teachers (classroom, RFF, support) is necessary to design and deliver units and lessons with an integrated, co-teaching approach to supporting all students			
6. **Case Management Approach**			
Putting FACES on the data using the case management approach is a two-pronged process: • **PREVENTION:** the co-construction of Data Walls allows staff members to stand back and discuss students' areas of need, to set targets, and to decide what is possible for each FACE, and • **INTERVENTION:** case management meetings (CMM's) in which a teacher presents one student at a time, through a work sample, to a problem-solving forum focused on supporting the classroom teacher with a recommended instructional strategy to try.			

Parameter	Delivering	Sustaining & Growing	Excelling
7. **Focused Professional Learning at Staff Meetings**			
• Using meeting times for Professional Learning builds teacher and leader collective capacity and develops a common language across all learning areas. • Starting with data, teachers who are Knowledgeable Others and leaders together provide the Professional Learning needed at staff meetings, Team meetings, modelling a culture of learning—The Third Teacher, that reflects clear expectations about precision in practice.			
8. **In-School Meetings—Collaborative Assessment of Work**			
It is often noted that the greatest variation in teaching in a system is not between schools; it is between classrooms in the same school. To reduce that variation, evidence of learning through student work samples is used in regular, ongoing co-teaching conversations in which teachers collaboratively determine: • How to sharpen their use of assessment data, every minute, to drive precise instruction; broaden their individual and collective instructional repertoire; • Challenge assumptions in a respectful way; • Improve immediate Descriptive Feedback strategies; • Move students from one level of work to the next and beyond expectations.			

(Continued)

(Continued)

Parameter	Delivering	Sustaining & Growing	Excelling
9. **Book Rooms of Levelled and Multi-Modal Resources**			
• Resources that support differentiated instruction are compiled and organised in a multimedia room or resources centre for teachers' access to just-right, just-in-time resources. • These high-quality, multi-modal resources reflect the diversity of the community, meet a range of abilities and needs, and address a range of student interests.			
10. **Allocation of System and School Budgets for Learning.**			
• Principals and leadership teams intentionally allocate budget items for resources that address instructional needs revealed by school and classroom assessment data. • Leaders can articulate why they are doing what they are choosing to do. Equity of outcomes for all learners is assured through budget resourcing (human and material) to support learning and learners.			
11. **Collaborative Inquiry—A Whole System Approach**			
• Every system or school meeting begins with a review of data, searching for the impact of actions taken on previously identified issues. Questions about the data are the basis of SMART goals. Collaborative Inquiry (CI) questions follow and are developed by system leaders, principals and groups of teachers to test pedagogical approaches they feel will enable instruction to elevate student achievement to meet their collective SMART goals. • Development of CI questions is deliberate using a structured, collaboratively planned approach; it is not left to system teams or schools to independently create their own processes because "being systematic" counts.			

Parameter	Delivering	Sustaining & Growing	Excelling
12. Parental and Community Involvement			
• Research indicates that parent and community increase all students' achievement. Schools build strong relationships with parents by keeping them informed about their children's progress and by involving them in the why and how the school is teaching literacy skills, for example, in every subject area. • Parents, caregivers and the broader community are helped to understand how they can support their children and are continuously invited to provide input into annual system and plans for improvement.			
13. Cross Curricular Literacy Connections			
• Assessment data determine what literacy skills each student will need to develop in order to access a subject's curriculum content; however, teachers in all content areas can further students' achievement by modelling the skills, sharing in the making of meaning, guiding students toward independence, and monitoring their independent work using the Gradual Release and Acceptance of Responsibility model in all subject areas.			
14. Shared Responsibility and Accountability			
• Everyone is responsible and accountable for every learner within and across schools in a district and state. That is, everyone knows and can clearly articulate the system, school, and classroom priority because SMART Goals and CI questions are aligned, clear, precise, intentional, and published. • Everyone sees himself or herself as responsible for achieving the goals and accountable for the learning that results from their implementation.			

Source: Created by Melissa Kable. Used with permission.

professional assessment and instructional practices were making a difference to the FACES. Listening and supporting the conversations, asking the right clarifying questions about concerns, and suggesting possible solutions led to greater understanding and increased intra-classroom collaboration.

The most recent Data Walls (Figure 8.3) have photos of students on Data Cards (Figure 8.4) in their class color (e.g., Kinder – Blue, Year 1 – Green, Year 2 – Teal, Year 3 – Jade, etc.); aboriginal students are identified with a hand; capital A signals Attendance issues; and an arrow up, arrow down or = indicates above, at, or below expectation. The staff tracked students' growth and achievement. Students who completed NAPLAN have a sticker showing their NAPLAN scoring band. Each photo also has a QR code linking to the Essential Assessment Maths online platform KVPS uses, which also stores the completed Case Management Meeting templates. Every tag on the Data Wall tells a broad story about each FACE. The data cards support very rich Data Talks. Kable made a point, "When we first began, staff were excited to move the student data cards along the Data Wall to show their progress. Learning support staff could easily identify which students needed support. That excitement continues today at KVPS. Improved student outcomes are celebrated regularly during staff meetings. It is important for all staff to see the impact their improved practice is having. The improving data tells an amazing story: The improvements are real; they reward our focus on our research to discover 'Consistency.'"

After Kable presented Sharratt's research and rationale behind Learning Walks and Talks (LWTs) at a full staff meeting, the principal, middle leaders and Kable, engaged in regular LWTs in 2022 and 2023. During the PL, staff learned that LWTs were an instructional leadership tool to "drive a cycle of continuous improvement by focusing on the effects of assessment that informs instruction." (Sharratt, 2019). Kable said, "Staff listened intently to expectations, and protocols were established to ensure consistency in implementation, including the fact that LWTs were non-evaluative. All staff were invited to do LWTs with leaders and colleagues and, after many LWTs in classrooms, they provided authentic, specific feedback to each other."

After many LWT's, teachers completed an online reflection to determine how it was going. This included an assessment of student engagement, evidence of Learning Intentions and Success Criteria (LI/SC) and what they heard when they asked students the 5 Questions. (Sharratt, 2019, p. 332).

Figure 8.3 Co-constructed Data Walls

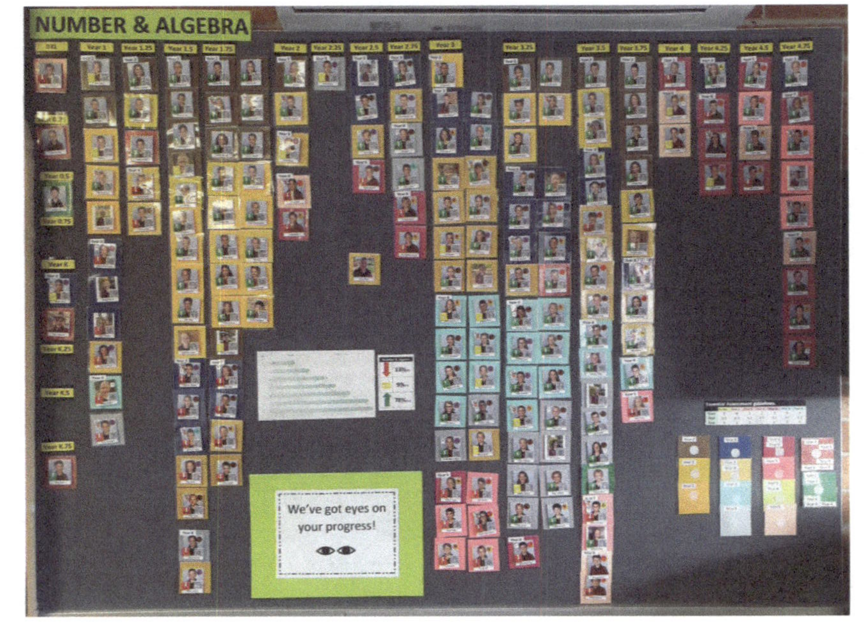

(Continued)

(Continued)

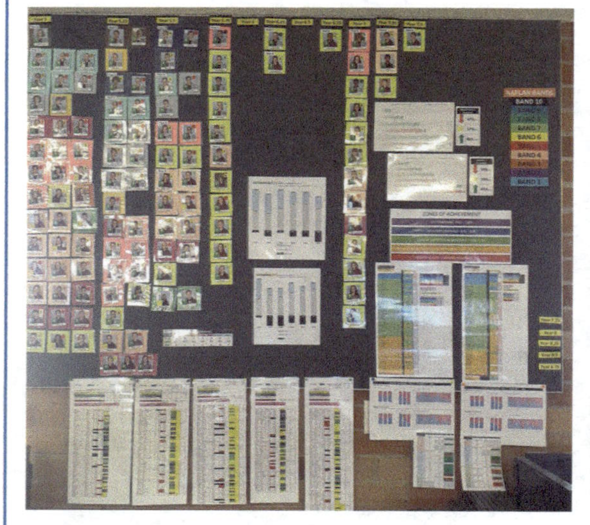

Source: Created by Melissa Kable. Used with permission.

Figure 8.4 Sample Data Card

Source: Created by Melissa Kable. Used with permission.

1. What are you learning? Why?
2. How are you doing?
3. How do you know?
4. How can you improve?
5. Where do you go for help?

Evidence of listening was reflected in students' responses to the questions. Kable said the learning for staff came from determining together that "Some students could tell the LWT teachers about the Learning Intentions/Success Criteria, the elements of the Third Teacher in their classroom, and where they could go for help beyond the teacher. Others needed prompting. This directed teachers to become more precise in their practice to ensure students understood the 5 Questions (Sharratt, Chapter 2, 2019) and became 'assessment capable learners.' (Frey et al., 2018). Teachers realized the ability to answer the 5 Questions was linked to the Assessment Waterfall Chart (CLARITY, p. 124), which became a focus for Reflective Practice in teams, a process which added precision and depth in their teaching."

Kable and the principal listened empathically as staff voiced concerns about using Release from Face to Face (RFF) time for LWTs. As an "off-class" assistant principal, Kable was able to respond by supporting staff. She chose to teach classes so teachers could participate in LWTs.' In 2024, LWTs began again with leaders and teachers walking in classrooms and reflecting on what they heard from students in order to collect data on their next steps in PL.

"Parents and caregivers were involved in the CLARITY approach," Kable said When attending school interviews, parents were provided with laminated copies of "The 5 Questions Parents Can Ask Their Child" (Sharratt, 2019, Chapter 2) to pop on the fridge and use to prompt discussion with their children."

5 QUESTIONS PARENTS CAN ASK THEIR CHILDREN

1. What did you learn today?
2. How did you go/do?
3. What did you do if you didn't understand?
4. How can you improve on your learning?
5. What are you most proud of?

KVPS went further in dialogue with parents and caregivers by publishing "The 5 Questions Parents Can Ask Their Child's Teacher" in the school newsletter as a response to parents and carers who indicated they were sometimes unsure of what to ask their child's teacher.

5 QUESTIONS PARENTS CAN ASK TEACHERS

1. What is my child learning? Why is s/he learning it?
2. How is s/he doing?
3. How do you know (how s/he is doing)?
4. How can s/he improve?
5. What supports can I provide, and can you provide if s/he is struggling? When will we check in again?

Kable added, "These questions were a starting point both for families to improve how they listen to their children and for teachers to listen to families about their children, recognizing that parents are a student's 'first teacher.'"

STAFF "BUY-IN"?

As 2023 ended, KVPS staff reflected on their ongoing plan to implement the 14 Parameters (Sharratt, 2019, page 11) as shown in Figure 8.5. In 2024, they are all continuing to work on this collaborative work with teachers and students.

IMPACT

Reporting on the results, Kable said, "We revisited the 14 Parameter Self-Assessment Tool regularly. By the end of 2023, we saw the red and yellow in every category as shown in Figure 8.6 had become yellow or green because of our focus on Consistency of impactful practice in every classroom. By completing the Tool in Stage teams, the teachers saw how the changes in their own assessments on the Tool were directly related to the increasingly positive results for all students, as shown in Figure 8.7 and Figure 8.8.

Figure 8.5 Visualizing the Ongoing *CLARITY* Work

CLARITY	2023 FOCUS	(Self-assessment in Term 4)
Parameter 3: Quality assessment informs instruction • Gradual Release and Acceptance of Responsibility (GRR) model	**Parameter 6:** Case Management Approach • Intervention: Case Management Meetings (CMM's)	**Parameter 7:** Focused professional learning • The Third Teacher
Parameter 8: In-school meetings – collaborative assessment of work • Descriptive Feedback strategies	**Parameter 11:** Collaborative Inquiry – A whole system approach • Collaborative Inquiry (CI)	**Parameter 13:** Cross Curricular literacy connections

Source: Created by Melissa Kable. Used with permission.

Kable concludes with a final assessment of Impact: "As a result of this focus on Consistency in implementing the 14 Parameters and our CLARITY research study together, our literacy and Numeracy data has been amazing. CLARITY has been a game changer for us (Figures 8.6 and 8.7)."

"A focus for the whole staff was Number and Algebra. Figure 8.8 indicates the percentage and number of students who showed growth (green arrow) from the pre- to post-assessment, stayed the same (equals sign), or showed no growth (red arrow). We already knew the FACES of these students as they were on our Data Wall photos." This impressive improvement shows how listening, collaboration, and the co-construction of meaning impacts a student's growth and achievement in very tangible ways."

Figure 8.6 The 14 Parameter Self-Assessment Tool Revisited

14 Parameters Self-assessment Tool		Term 1	2022			Term 4	2022			Term 4	2023
Parameter	D	S & G	E		D	S & G	E		D	S & G	E
1. Shared Beliefs and Understanding											
2. Embedded Knowledgeable Others											
3. Quality Assessment Informs Instruction											
4. Principal as Lead Learner											
5. Early and Ongoing Interventions											
6. Case Management Approach											
7. Focused Professional Learning at Staff Meetings											
8. In-School Meetings—Collaborative Assessment of Work											
9. Book Rooms of Levelled and Multi-Modal Resources											
10. Allocation of System and School Budgets for Learning											
11. Collaborative Inquiry—A Whole System Approach											
12. Parental and Community Involvement											
13. Cross Curricular Literacy Connections											
14. Shared Responsibility and Accountability											

Source: Created by Melissa Kable. Used with permission.

Figure 8.7 2022 Improvement "In the Green"!

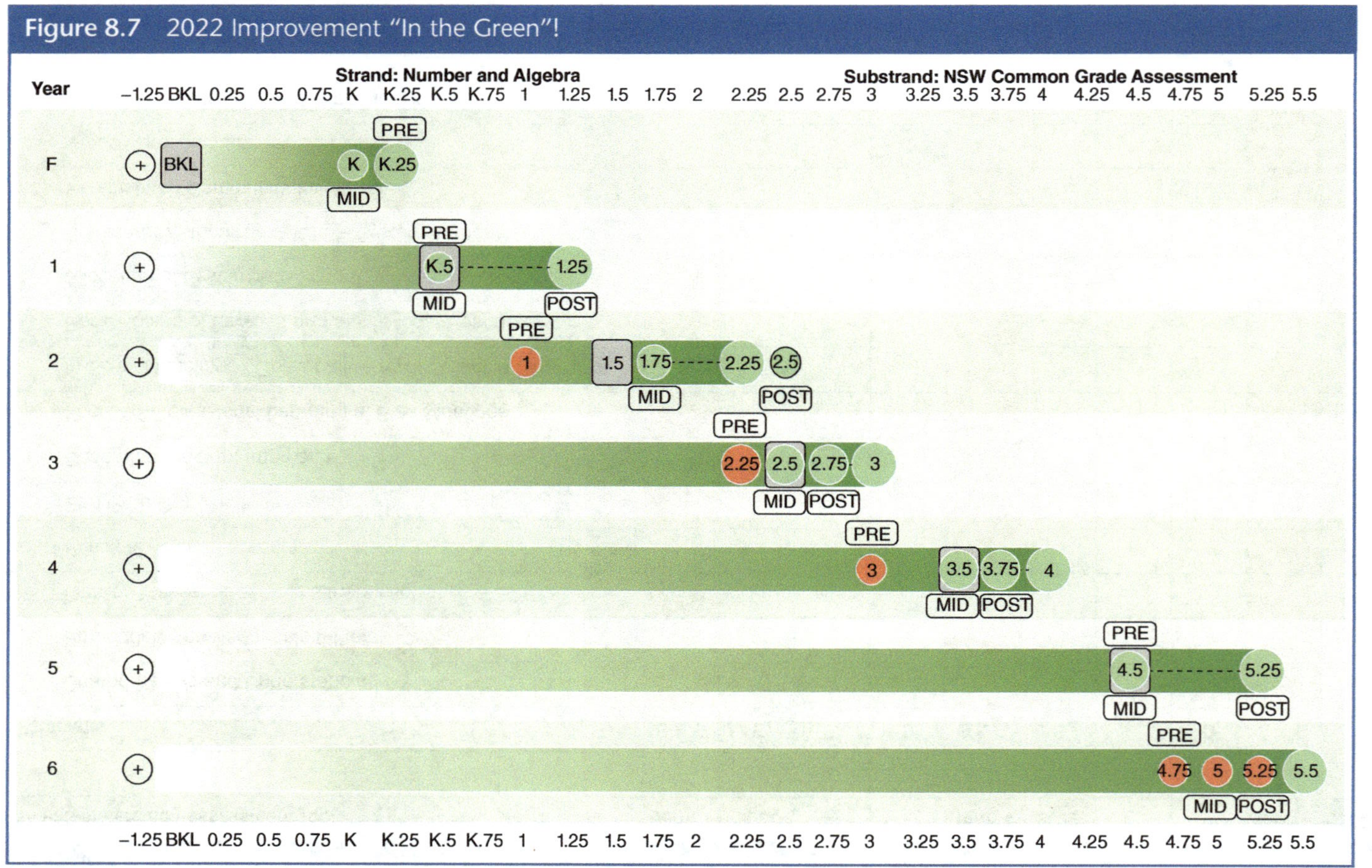

Source: Created by Melissa Kable. Used with permission.

Figure 8.8 Summary Graphic of Improvement

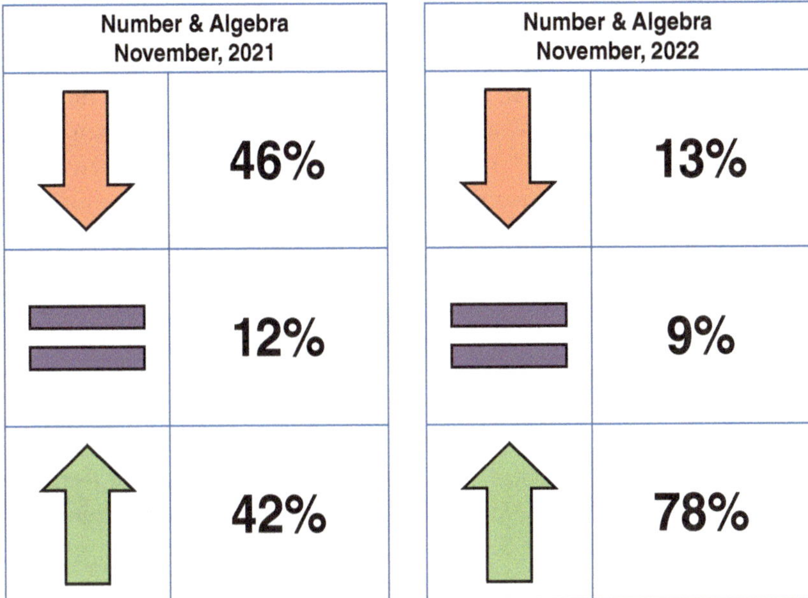

Source: Created by Melissa Kable. Used with permission.

LEADERSHIP LESSONS LEARNED

"Beginning our *CLARITY* adventure with the end in mind was essential," said staff members. Leaders listened to staff concerns about well-being post-COVID and involved staff collaboratively in making connections between the 14 Parameters and what they were already doing. The new work built upon the base of what staff already knew . . . it wasn't something completely new where everything had to be thrown out. Practical elements of CLARITY gave staff essential, simple, effective tools to use in the classroom, tools with which they could immediately see success. While the *CLARITY* content reflected in the Self-Assessment Tool scale showed growth among staff, and while growth and achievement of students across the school improved, there was a very noticeable increase in the level of collaboration across the staff. To get to that collaboration meant developing and sustaining Operating Norms for meetings, honestly **listening** to each other, and being willing and feeling enabled to ask questions and express fact-supported opinions. Staff realized the increased levels of real **listening** for understanding to the thinking expressed in conversations in PL sessions, at the Data Wall, and in Learning Walks and Talks fostered professionalism and interpersonal relationships across staff. They noted that improving their own **listening** skills resulted in modeling and teaching their students how to actively **listen** to each other. This, in addition to creating a consistent and relentless approach to embedding the 14 Parameters, ensured effective productivity in all areas of school life. Teacher pedagogy improved including co-constructing Success Criteria, creating The Third Teacher learning spaces, and engaging in LWTs. The enhanced "precision-in-practice" increased staff efficacy and positively impacted student learning outcomes as students had a better understanding and ownership of the curriculum expectations.

On reflection, staff and leaders reported that listening was essential throughout their *CLARITY* adventure. They created and still maintain a continuous culture of care, open communication and a safe learning environment everywhere. Staff felt heard and valued! Staff listened to students' responses to the 5 *CLARITY* questions, asking clarifying questions when needed. Students listened when co-constructing The Third Teacher spaces and Success Criteria with teachers. Staff have created an exemplary school in Central Coast, NSW.

As Gerry O'Brien wrote, "upon assuming the role of Principal at Killarney Vale, I was promptly informed of the school's comprehensive adoption of the *CLARITY* approach. Having encountered *CLARITY* only briefly in my previous school, I was particularly intrigued by its implementation at KVPS. Among my initial observations was the presentation of the Data Wall, where I encountered "putting FACES on the Data" feature. I was notably impressed by the ability to visually track the academic progress of every student in relation to Reading and Numeracy.

"Over the subsequent months, I witnessed firsthand the considerable benefits of monitoring student advancement these Data Walls in Literacy and Maths afforded. I actively engaged in the substantive discussions regularly convened between Mel Kable and the teaching staff. These discussions centred on students' current academic standing and strategic planning for their ongoing growth and development. The tangible impact of the *CLARITY* research became increasingly apparent as students progressed along the Data Walls, indicative of its efficacy and effectiveness.

"Furthermore, the enthusiastic endorsement from staff fostered a culture of consistency in teaching methodologies throughout the school. The collective commitment to *CLARITY* demonstrated by both the outcomes achieved and the staff's engagement underscores its significance within the school community, affirming its necessity for continuity."

SUMMARY

Kable concluded, "I have found/we have found that *CLARITY* is just so easy to use. Staff have embraced the new learning and find it so practical and useful for best classroom practice. To see the FACES on the Data Walls and know teachers can speak and will be listened to inspires a willingness to share concerns. This culture of learning provides the foundation for subsequent sharing of instructional strategies between teachers—Attend, Hear, and Understand for the benefit of students who are at risk, and, coincidentally for all kids in the class [I Appraise and Activate]. Finally Kable noted, "To have conversations around a shared focus like consistency has helped us develop a common language of improvement as we go. We are doing some things differently from other schools, and we love what we're doing because it's working. Our data sources are telling us that. The shift in the last twelve months has been amazing." (See Figure 8.7).

LISTEN HERE!

Attentive listening is a responsibility of students, teachers and support teachers, school leaders at all levels, and system consultants and leaders. It is everyone's responsibility. The outcomes are everyone's rewards. Providing the group norms that support a culture in which it can and does occur is the responsibility of leaders. This narrative offered by KVPS is a gift to all of us as it talks to our listening progression (Attending, Hearing, Understanding, Appraising, and Activating) as a definite strategy for developing school or system improvement. Leaders and staff collaboratively undertook this improvement journey together by reading *CLARITY*, listening to each other, understanding and building on the ideas of others, making the time to discuss the "big ideas," and by implementing them—consistently! Thank you, Mel, Gerry, and staff from KVPS for sharing with us your incredibly positive journey.

DELIBERATE PAUSE

As demonstrated in the KVPS Case Study, building on the ideas of others is an adult listening skill that must be taught explicitly to students. A proven, practical strategy is to have students track, on a visual learning map, the different sentence starters they use to listen first and then build on the ideas of others. Some sample sentence stems that get us started on developing such a map include:

- ✓ I agree with Ryan and add . . .
- ✓ That is a great idea, Robbie, and . . .
- ✓ I disagree with Jackson's point (not, I disagree with Jackson) because . . .
- ✓ I hear Madeleine's point of view and want to build on it by saying . . .

Classroom anchor charts using sample sentence stems and continuously adding to them encourage students and teachers to use Accountable Listening and Talking prompts that take listening and thinking to a higher level. The ability to self-regulate by first listening for understanding—to build on the previous speaker's comments and then being able to move to a more satisfactory action or solution—is an outcome of intentional listening.

COMMITMENT

I commit to:

1. *Tracking the progression of students' listening skills from I Attend to I Hear, to I Understand, to I Appraise, to I Activate.*
2. *Being explicit in teaching and tracking sentence starters that students are using to listen and to build positively on the ideas of others.*
3. *Having students track their Accountable Listening and Talking skills.*
4. *Investigating what listening approaches works best in my (our) classroom(s) in our staff meetings.*

In our concluding chapter, we wrap up our thoughts, leaving the reader with exemplary practices that will impact teacher practice to make "listening" a priority for every learner.

CONCLUDING THOUGHTS

CHAPTER 9

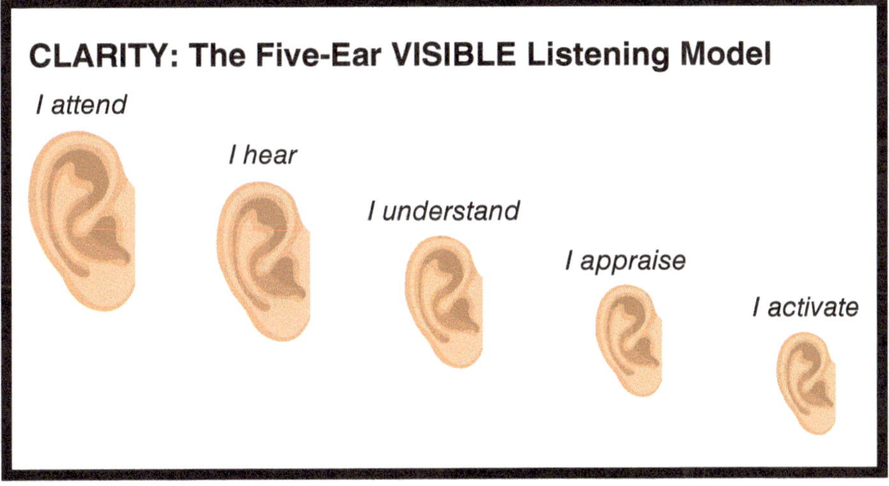

We are often asked: "What is the single most effective action you have taken, as leaders, to support teachers and students?"

Firstly, we would say that leaders need to be seen to be creating and sustaining an environment that enables and encourages listening, hearing, and responding in a "build upon" way. Whether the listening, hearing, and responding is to new ideas/concepts or to responses from other staff, community members or students, the first step in leading is developing that positive listening-learning culture. It sets up the system, school, or class for success in their collaborative learning processes.

Secondly, we would say determining direction together by asking: "Where are we going?" This is the ultimate end point leaders and teachers need to have in mind whenever they are beginning system and school improvement. Beginning with the end in mind, we note that feedback is so often talked about in terms of the nature, timing, and quality of the feedback provided (Effect Size of Quality Feedback: .70, Hattie, 2016), and we forget that it is of no value if it is not heard, understood, and actioned. The aim is to teach students to attend, hear, understand, appraise, and action the feedback they receive on their work. That is, feedback provided by teachers or peers against the co-constructed Success Criteria (Effect Size .88, Hattie & Clarke, 2018).

Similarly, the aim with teacher clarity (Effect Size: .70 Hattie, 2016) is to have them feel they too can safely give and get feedback on their work. Teachers must be able to attend, hear, respond, appraise the feedback given and act on it. With students and with teachers, the purpose is the same—namely, to build on quality feedback so that leaders and staff can improve the life chances of students in their care, raising the sense of self efficacy of *all* (Effect Size: 1.57, Hattie & Clarke, 2018).

For example, English et al. (2023) specifically write, "In the Scottish reform context, teachers are called on to enhance student conceptual understanding by 'us[ing] student misconceptions and wrong answers,' implying student struggle (Curriculum for Excellence Scotland CFES, 2012, p. 2). Additionally, the Scotland *Mathematics Excellence Group's* (2011) report on instructional changes needed to make said reforms effective, recommends that teachers change *how* they listen from an 'evaluative' form of listening—that assesses the correctness of student answers—to 'interpretive listening' focused on understanding student thinking (p. 10)."

In English et al.'s study (2023), teachers' practices of pedagogical listening was supported by a cultivated disposition to listen to all children's expression of struggle. They called this a "listening stance" (Schultz, 2003). Extending Schultz's (2003) definition, English et al. consider a listening stance to mean being prepared to listen to, respond responsibly to, and *be with*, all learners as their thinking and struggle emerges. They conclude that teacher education and professionalization must support teachers in cultivating complex modes of listening that they have brought together under the concept of pedagogical listening.

We constantly observe that leaders who hear, listen and check for understanding are modeling and inviting "open-to-learning stance" and an "openly caring stance." Now we conclude that ***all*** leaders and teachers must have an "open-to-listening stance". No matter what their position in a system or school, their listening creates a learning environment—a positive culture of care and concern for others that shows others that they embrace differing points of view. It's not just that they listen intently and establish a culture of trust and learning; they use their leadership skills to establish a vision with agreed-upon steps and measures of success for teachers, staff and/or students. Importantly, they get on with facilitating positive decisions on "what resources and PL do we need to mobilize?", and "how will we support each other to accomplish our intended goals?"

"Intentional Listening" and the ensuing dialogue are instrumental in having teachers feel that their voices are heard and that their thoughts are valued. As teachers, we appreciate, most, leaders who listen and become learners themselves. These leaders:

- Engage in a dialogue of "no excuses," focusing directly on the moral imperative of believing "all students can learn" and "all teachers can teach";
- Select Knowledgeable Others (KOs) from among the most respected, credible classroom teachers to walk alongside them, learning from these KOs by asking authentic questions, practicing what they have heard and then continuing to reflect on their own next steps in learning;
- Provide focused time and relevant resources to support teachers' efforts to embed precision-in-practice in every elementary and secondary classroom;
- Identify and share teachers' "remarkable moments," especially following seemingly impossible learning growth gains;
- Establish innovative and responsive cultures of growth characterized by relational trust; and
- Model the importance of listening to and celebrating others' successes.

Leaders who listen for understanding hear and activate the best answers to these questions:

- Do we open classroom doors to make teaching and learning public?
- Do we build a caring community of learners, which includes parents and the broader community as partners?
- By doing what we're doing, do we create a "we-we" culture of learning where there is responsibility and accountability for all students within and across schools?
- Do we create a trusting and respectful learning environment where students and teachers feel safe to take risks, to make mistakes—and where mistakes are seen as learning opportunities?
- Do we develop and leave many more leaders behind to continue the achievement work when we are gone? Can we be easily and seamlessly replaced?
- Do we ensure transparency, accountability, and ownership by all for achieving the desired results?
- Do we confront our own biases and challenge those of others?

In sum, as leaders and teachers transforming a culture of learning, focused on assessment that improves instruction in our schools, we are ***all*** called upon to use the elements of the interdependent CLARITY: The Five-Ear VISIBLE Listening Model to achieve the highest level of professional skill that we can perfect for ourselves and others. Our goal in doing so is to increase teachers' capacity to teach ***all*** students to become our critically listening graduates—the key to society's future health and well-being.

COMMITMENT

I commit to:

1. *Learning how to use the elements of the 5 Ear Model of Listening within my leadership and classroom practice. I will become better at and continually be aware of my impact as "I attend. I hear, I understand, I appraise, I activate."*
2. *Setting up the conditions in which others I lead will learn to both use the 5 Ear model elements and respect others using them.*
3. *Making these elements of listening a key and visible part of my leadership style—not at the expense of achieving student growth and achievement—but as the cornerstone of my leadership strategy to make our system, networks, schools and classrooms be the best they can for our students and staff.*

Giving it "a go"!

EPILOGUE

I am honored to be invited by John Hattie and Lyn Sharratt to write the epilogue of their new book *Learning to Listen and Listening to Learn: Empowering Visible Clarity*. In this book, John and Lyn examine the importance and impact of listening in the classroom. Two-way communication is central to teaching and learning. Listening is the basis of two-way communication. The better we listen, the better we learn. This point seems so elementary and yet in reality so profound and difficult to practice! Good listening is a critical skill in helping a learner expand his or her learning capacity. This book provides us with a fascinating account of how teachers can help students improve their proficiency in listening and therefore learn better. Teachers are also encouraged to improve their own listening skills. If teachers do not listen, how do they understand their students and their students' learning difficulties?

The lessons in the book are beneficial to those who are directly involved in the classroom. I will not repeat them. But they are equally applicable in educational policymaking and school leadership. I teach educational leaders in Singapore regarding policy, leadership, and educational change. Often, communication is regarded as one of the biggest leadership challenges. In teaching this area of work, I have a little tagline: "Don't think communication. Think pedagogy!" What I mean is that an aspect of good pedagogy is that teachers seek to connect with students by articulating the teaching points in a way that students can relate to and understand easily. When we communicate as leaders or policy makers, we can and should use the same principle. Communication is not just about preparing a set of slides to be read.

But this book has reminded me of something more fundamental about my tagline. Communication is two-way. We should seek to articulate better. More importantly, we should seek to listen better. Better articulation makes listening easier, but it is better listening on both sides that enhances mutual understanding and builds relationships. If we start with an attitude of not wanting to listen, communication will break down even with the most sophisticated manner of articulation. The more I read this book, I more I am reminded of "talk less, listen more." I am a teacher. As a teacher, I tend to talk more than I listen. It is an occupational hazard or probably just a convenient excuse. I think I should do better, not just in the workplace but even at home! Did my wife just applaud?

Many years ago, when I was a very young teacher, I was a social work volunteer and did some youth counseling. One day I met this boy. He was probably thirteen or fourteen years old. He was missing classes and spending time with a street gang outside school. He was not my student, nor was he my direct counselee. It was just a chance meeting, but I had heard a few things about his misdeeds.

I spoke with him and essentially told him that he should be attending school regularly and not mixing with bad company. Of course, he was not happy with what I was saying, but he did not argue with me. He tried to say something, but I thought I knew what he was going to say. So, I told him "I understand, but . . ." and carried on saying all the "right" things that caring adults were supposed to say. He tried to say something again, but again I cut him short with "I understand, but. . .". All these typical excuses of teenagers—I thought I had heard them all.

Then, he became really upset. He put up his hand and asked me to stop. He said, "Let me ask you something first. You are a teacher now, yes? You have a degree?"

Strange question. I said "yes."

"Pay is good?"

"Well, not too bad . . ." could always be better, I thought.

"I see . . . when you were in school, your parents gave you pocket money?"

"Yes . . ." I really wondered where he was going with this.

Then he pointed at my nose and said to me, "do you know who you are?"

My response was probably a blank stare and "huh?"

He said to me, "you are a person who is born lucky, OK? I am not. You can study. I can't. Your parents gave you money. I don't have such parents."

"Do you know that my father is in jail? My mother—I don't know where she is. For every cent that I spend now, I earned it, borrowed it, or stole it. So, stop saying you understand me. Don't pretend to understand me. You are not even interested in listening to me."

I was stunned and did not know what to say. There was pain and anger in his voice. In fact, you could guess that in writing this, I have modified his language to make it suitable for this book. In that moment, there was no escape from the truth. I did not understand him. *I wasn't listening.* I was just lecturing him from my own high pedestal. I thought I was there to educate him. I was educated instead.

Maybe the reason he mixed with the street gang was because he could not find acceptance anywhere else. Not in class. Not in school. If you are a teacher, maybe you have a couple of students like him. They seem to have lost all interest in studies and have given up on themselves. But please do not give up on them. *Listen to their story.* That may be the best gift to them. You may not be able to change their life circumstances. Listening may be the only thing that you can do for them. It may also be the best thing that you can do for them. When you listen, there is a connection. From that connection, students can draw strength and courage to overcome their own challenges. The message of this book has hit home with Visible Clarity. Sometimes, the best gift that we can offer another person is the gift of listening. I wish everyone who reads this book all the best in listening both more and better!

Pak Tee Ng, PhD
Nanyang Technical University
Singapore

REFERENCES AND FURTHER READINGS

Alexander, R. (2001). *Culture and pedagogy: International comparisons in primary education.* Blackwell.

Alexander, R. (2020). *A dialogic teaching companion.* Routledge.

Anderson, R. C., Chinn, C., Waggoner, M., & Nguyen, K. (1998). Intellectually stimulating story discussions. In J. Osborn & F. Lehr (Eds.), *Literacy for all: Issues in teaching and learning* (pp. 170–186). Guilford Publications.

Asay, L. D., & Orgill, M. (2010). Analysis of essential features of inquiry found in articles published in The Science Teacher, 1998–2007. *Journal of Science Teacher Education, 21*(1), 57–79.

Bandura, A. (1986). *Social foundations of thought and action.* Prentice-Hall.

Beck, I. L., McKeown, M. G., & Sandora, C. A. (2020). *Robust comprehension instruction with questioning the author: 15 years smarter.* Guilford Publications.

Berne, J. E. (1998). Examining the relationship between L2 listening research, pedagogical theory, and practice. *Foreign Language Annals, 31,* 169–190.

Berninger, V. W., & Abbott, R. D. (2010). Listening comprehension, oral expression, reading comprehension, and written expression: Related yet unique language systems in grades 1, 3, 5, and 7. *Journal of Educational Psychology, 102*(3), 635.

Boaler, J., & Brodie, K. (2004). The importance, nature and impact of teacher questions. In D. E. McDougall & J. A. Ross (Eds.), *Proceedings of the twenty-sixth annual meeting of the North American Chapter of the International Group for the Psychology of Mathematics Education* (Vol. 2, pp. 774–782). OISE/UT.

Bodie, G. D., & Fitch-Hauser, M. (2010). Quantitative research in listening: Explication and overview. In A. D. Wolvin (Ed.), *Listening and human communication in the 21st century* (pp. 46–93). Wiley.

Bodie, G. D., Worthington, D., & Fitch-Hauser, M. (2011). A comparison of four measurement models for the Watson–Barker Listening Test (WBLT)–Form C. *Communication Research Reports, 28*(1), 32–42.

Bostrom, R. N., & Bryant, C. L. (1980). Factors in the retention of information presented orally: The role of short-term listening. *Western Journal of Communication, 44*(2), 137–145.

Bowers, L., Huisingh, R., & LoGiudice, C. (2009). *The listening comprehension test—Adolescence.* LinguiSystems, Inc; East Moline.

Brandao, S., Cadime, I., Ribeiro, I., & Viana, F. L. (2014). Evaluating listening comprehension in children using a dynamic assessment approach: An exploratory study. *European Journal of Developmental Psychology, 11*(6), 746–753.

Brimer, A. (2002). *Word meaning through listening*. Educational Evaluations.

Brunsman, B. A., & Person, C. M. (2014). *Oral and written language scales* (2nd ed.). Western Psychological Services.

Buber, M. [1925] 1986) Über das Erzieherische, in Reden über Erziehung (7th edn), Heidelberg: Lambert Schneider.

Buber, M. (1965). *The knowledge of man: Selected essays* (M. S. Friedman & C. R. Rogers, Eds.). Humanity Books.

Buck, G. (2001). *Assessing listening*. Cambridge University Press.

Burry, P. J. (2008). *Living with "The Gloria films:" A daughter's memory*. PCCS Books.

Carrow-Woolfolk, E. (1995). *Oral and written language scales* (Vol. 93). American Guidance Service.

Celce-Murcia, M., Dörnyei, Z., & Thurrell, S. (1995). Communicative competence: A pedagogically motivated model with content specifications. *Issues in Applied Linguistics, 6*(2), 5–35.

Chiles, M. (2023). *Powerful questioning: Strategies for improving learning and retention in the classroom*. Crown House Publishing Ltd.

Chion, M. (1994). *Audio-vision: Sound on screen*. Columbia University Press.

Claxton, G. (2014). The development of learning power: A new perspective on child development and early education. In S. Robson & S. F. Quinn (Eds.), *The Routledge international handbook of young children's thinking and understanding* (pp. 367–376). Routledge.

Clinton, J., & Dawson, G. (2018). Enfranchising the profession through evaluation: A story from Australia. *Teachers and Teaching, 24*(3), 312–327.

Covey, S. R. (2020). *The 7 habits of highly effective people*. Simon & Schuster.

CTB Macmillan/McGraw-Hill. (1993). *Listening and speaking checklist*. Author.

Darr, C., Ferral, H., Twist, J., & Watson, V. (2008). *PAT (Progressive Achievement Test) – Reading comprehension: Revised 2008*. NZCER.

DeWitt, P. M. (2020). *Instructional leadership: Creating practice out of theory*. Corwin.

English, A. R., Tyson, K., Hintz, A., Murdoch, D., & Anderson, J. (2023, Oct. 19). Pedagogical listening: Understanding how teachers listen to student struggle during mathematical sense-making discussions. Teachers and Teaching, DOI: 10.1080/13540602.2023.2263738

Erdogan, I., & Campbell, T. (2008). Teacher questioning and interaction patterns in classrooms facilitated with differing levels of constructivist teaching practices. *International Journal of Science Education, 30*(14), 1891–1914.

Flanders, N. A. (1965). *Teacher influence, pupil attitudes, and achievement: Ned A. Flanders (No. 12)*. US Department of Health, Education, and Welfare, Office of Education.

Flowerdew, J., & Miller, L. (2005). *Second language listening: Theory and practice.* Cambridge University Press.

Fontana, P. C., Cohen, S. D., & Wolvin, A. D. (2015). Understanding listening competency: A systematic review of research scales. *International Journal of Listening, 29*(3), 148–176.

Frey, N., Hattie, J., & Fisher, D. (2018). *Developing assessment capable learners.* Corwin.

Galton, M. J. (1995). *Crisis in the primary classroom.* D. Fulton Publishers.

Geffner, D. S., & Ross-Swain, D. (2006). *The listening inventory.* Academic Therapy Publications.

Gilson, C. M., Flowers, C., & Chang, W.-H. (2024). The teacher listening orientation questionnaire: A validity study. *International Journal of Listening, 38*(3), 231–245.

Goodwin, A. P., Petscher, Y., Jones, S., McFadden, S., Reynolds, D., & Lantos, T. (2020). The monster in the classroom: Assessing language to inform instruction. *The Reading Teacher, 73*(5), 603–616.

Gough, P. B., & Tunmer, W. (1986). Decoding, reading, and reading disability. *Remedial and Special Education, 7,* 6–10.

Guenther, K. (2022). "Um, mm-h, yeah": Carl Rogers, phonographic recordings, and the making of therapeutic listening. *History of Psychology, 25*(3), 191.

Hagues, N., Siddiqui, R., & Merwood, P. (1999). *Listening comprehension test series.* National Foundation for Educational Research.

Hargreaves, L., & Galton, M. (2002). *Transfer from the primary classroom.* Routledge.

Hattie, J. (1978). *The development of a telephone listening and referral service.* UNE.

Hattie, J., & Clarke, S. (2018). *Visible learning: Feedback.* Routledge.

Hattie, J., Fisher, D., Frey, N., & Clarke, S. (2021). *Collective student efficacy: Developing independent and inter-dependent learners.* Corwin.

Hattie, J., & Hamilton, A. (2018). *Cargo cults must die.* https://www.visiblelearningplus.com/groups/cargo-cults-must-die-white-paper

Hattie, J., O'Leary, T., Hattie, K., & Donoghue, G. (2024). *Great learners by design: Principles and practices to supercharge learners.* Corwin.

Hattie, J.A.C. (2023). Foreword in Chiles, M. (2023). *Powerful questioning: Strategies for improving learning and retention in the classroom.* Crown House Publishing Ltd.

Imhof, M. (2010). What is going on in the mind of a listener? The cognitive psychology of listening. In A. D. Wolvin (Ed.), *Listening and human communication in the 21st century* (pp. 97–126). Wiley.

Imhof, M. (2016). Listening is easy!? Looking at critical factors for listening performance. In K. M. Carragee & A. Moennich (Eds.), *Communication as performance and the performativity of communication. Proceedings of the 2014 international colloquium on communication* (pp. 76–88). Virginia Tech. https://scholar.lib.vt.edu/ejournals/ICC/2014/ICC2014Imhof.pdf

Imhof, M. (2020). Psychology. In D. Worthington & G. Bodie (Eds.), *Handbook of listening* (pp. 234–253). Wiley.

Imhof, M., & Schlag, M. (2016). Fostering listening and learning in the classroom across the curriculum. *Listening Education, 6.*

International Listening Association. (1995). *ILA.* https://www.listen.org/

Itzchakov, G., Weinstein, N., Leary, M., Saluk, D., & Amar, M. (2024). Listening to understand: The role of high-quality listening on speakers' attitude depolarization during disagreements. *Journal of Personality and Social Psychology, 126*(2), 213–239. https://doi.org/10.1037/pspa0000366

Izumi, S. (2003). Processing difficulty in comprehension and production of relative clauses by learners of English as a second language. *Language Learning, 53*(2), 285–323.

Ji, S., Qin, X., & Li, K. (2022). A systematic review of foreign language listening anxiety: Focus on the theoretical definitions and measurements. *Frontiers in Psychology, 13,* Article 859021.

Jones, J. E., & Mohr, L. (1976). *The Jones-Mohr listening test.* John Wiley & Sons.

Jones, S. M. (2011). Supportive listening. *The International Journal of Listening, 25*(1–2), 85–103.

Kalinec-Craig, C. A. (2017). The rights of the learner: A framework for promoting equity through formative assessment in mathematics education. *Democracy and Education, 25*(2), Article 5. https://democracyeducationjournal.org/home/vol25/iss2/

Kane, T. J., McCaffrey, D. F., Miller, T., & Staiger, D. O. (2013). *Have we identified effective teachers? Validating measures of effective teaching using random assignment* (Research Paper). MET Project. Bill & Melinda Gates Foundation.

Kapur, M. (2024). *Productive failure: Unlocking deeper learning through the science of failing.* Synopsis.

Keith, N., & Frese, M. (2008). Effectiveness of error management training: A meta-analysis. *Journal of Applied Psychology, 93*(1), 59.

Kluger, A. N., & Itzchakov, G. (2022). The power of listening at work. *Annual Review of Organizational Psychology and Organizational Behavior, 9,* 121–146.

Kluger, A. N., & Mizrahi, M. (2023). Defining listening: Can we get rid of the adjectives? *Current Opinion in Psychology, 52,* Article 101639.

Lefstein, A., & Snell, J. (2011). Classroom discourse: The promise and complexity of dialogic practice. In S. Ellis & E. McCartney (Eds.), *Applied linguistics and primary school teaching* (pp. 165–185). Cambridge University Press.

Lloyd, P., Peers, I., & Foster, C. (2001). The listening skills test-a new instrument to assess children's pragmatic ability. *International Journal of Language & Communication Disorders, 36*(S1), 429–434.

Lynch, T., & Mendelsohn, D. (2013). Listening. In N. Schmitt (Ed.), *An introduction to applied linguistics* (pp. 190–206). Routledge.

Martin, N., Brownell, R., & Hamaguchi, P. (2018). *TAPS-4: A language processing skills assessment.* Western Psychological Services.

Mathieson, K. (2007). *Identifying special needs in the early years.* SAGE.

Meek, M. (2012). *Learning to read.* Random House.

Meikle, T. (2016) *Blog post: Making thinking audible – A whole school approach.* www.thelearningexchange.ca

Mendelsohn, D. J. (1984). There ARE strategies for listening. TEAL Occasional Papers, 8, 63–76.

Mercer, N., Hennessy, S., & Warwick, P. (2019). Dialogue, thinking together and digital technology in the classroom: Some educational implications of a continuing line of inquiry. *International Journal of Educational Research, 97,* 187–199.

Michaels, S., O'Connor, C., & Resnick, L. B. (2008). Deliberative discourse idealized and realized: Accountable talk in the classroom and in civic life. *Studies in Philosophy and Education, 27*(4), 283–297.

Mills, E. P. (1974). *Listening: Key to communication.* Petrocelli.

Nelson-Jones, R. (2014). *Practical counselling and helping skills.* SAGE.

Nuthall, G. (2007). *The hidden lives of learners.* New Zealand Council for Education Research Press.

Nystrand, M., Gamoran, A., & Carbonaro, W. (1998). *Towards an ecology of learning: The case of classroom discourse and its effects on writing in high school English and social studies* (Report Series 2.34). National Research Center on English Learning & Achievement.

Nystrand, M., Wu, L. L., Gamoran, A., Zeiser, S., & Long, D. A. (2003). Questions in time: Investigating the structure and dynamics of unfolding classroom discourse. *Discourse Processes, 35*(2), 135–198.

Ontario Curriculum, Grades 1–8 Language. (2023). The King's Printer: Toronto, Ontario, Canada.

Ontario Ministry of Education. (2004). Literacy for learning: Report of the expert panel on literacy in grades 4 to 6 in Ontario. Queen's Printer. *A Guide to Effective Literacy instruction,* Vol. I Grades 4–6.

Ontario Ministry of Education. (2011). *Having grand conversation in every classroom.*

Oxford, R. (2019). Teaching and researching listening skills: Theory-and research-based practices. In N. Polat, T. Gregersen, & P. D. MacIntyre (Eds.), *Research-driven pedagogy: Implications of L2A theory and research for the teaching of language skills* (pp. 10–34). Routledge. (Oxford, 1993; in Osada, 2004).

Paul, R., & Elder, L. (2007). Critical thinking: The art of Socratic questioning. *Journal of Developmental Education, 31*(1), 36–37.

Perls, F. S. (1969). *Gestalt therapy verbatim.* Real People Press.

Piaget, J. (1952). *The origins of intelligence.* International University Press.

Preiss, R. W., & Wheeless, L. R. (1989). Affective responses in listening: A meta-analysis of receiver apprehension outcomes. *International Journal of Listening, 3*(1), 72–102.

Psych Tests. (2011). *Listening skills inventory.* Author.

Psychological Corporation. (1993). *The classroom communication skills inventory listening and speaking checklist.* Author.

Randolph, J. (2007). Meta-analysis of the research on response cards: Efects on test achievement, quiz achievement, participation, and of-task behaviour. *Journal of Positive Behavioral Interventions, 9*(2), 113–128.

Raphael, T. E., Florio-Ruane, S., & George, M. (2001). Book club "plus": A conceptual framework to organize literacy instruction. *Language Arts, 79*(2), 159–168.

Reid, N., Johnson, I. C., & Elley, W. B. (2015) *PAT: Listening comprehension.* NZCER.

Rogers, C. R. (1951). *Client-centered therapy: Its current practice, implication, theory.* Houghton Mifflin.

Rogers, C. R. (1961). *On becoming a person.: A therapist's view of psychotherapy.* Houghton Mifflin.

Rogers, C. R. (1980). *A way of being.* Houghton Mifflin.

Roque, R., Rusk, N., & Resnick, M. (2016). Supporting diverse and creative collaboration in the Scratch online community. In U. Cress, J. Moskaliuk, & H. Jeong (Eds.), *Mass collaboration and education* (pp. 241–256). Springer.

Rost, M. (2020). Instructional design and assessment. In D. Worthington & G. Bodie (Eds.), *Handbook of listening* (pp. 265–278). Wiley.

Rowe, M. B. (1986). Wait time: Slowing down may be a way of speeding up. *Journal of Teacher Education, 37*(1), 43–50. http://sce4361-01.sp01.fsu.edu/waittime.html

Scardamalia, M., & Bereiter, C. (2006). Knowledge building: Theory, pedagogy, and technology. In K. Sawyer (Ed.), *Cambridge handbook of the learning sciences* (pp. 97–118). Cambridge University Press.

Schultz, K. (2003). *Listening: A framework for teaching across differences.* Teachers College Press.

Senge, P. (1990). *The fifth discipline. The art and practice of the learning organization.* Doubleday.

Sharratt, L. (1996). *Schools as learning organizations* [Unpublished doctoral thesis]. University of Toronto, Canada.

Sharratt, L. (2019). *CLARITY: What matters MOST in learning, teaching and leading.* Corwin.

Sharratt, L. (2023). *Research-into-practice that is solution-focused.* Catholic Principals' Counsel of Ontario.

Sharratt, L., & Fullan, M. (2009). *Realization: The change imperative for district-wide reform.* Corwin.

Sharratt, L., & Fullan, M. (2022). *Putting FACES on the data: What great leaders and teachers do!* Corwin.

Sharratt, L., & Harild, G. (2015). *Good to great to innovate: Recalculating the route, K-12.* Corwin.

Sharratt, L., & Planche, B. (2016). *Leading collaborative learning: Empowering excellence.* Corwin.

Shomoossi, N. (2004). The effect of teachers questioning behavior on EFL Classroom interaction: A classroom research study. *The Reading Matrix, 4*(2), 96–102.

Sizer, T. R. (2005). *The red pencil: Convictions from experience in education.* Yale University Press

Smith, F., Hardman, F., Wall, K., & Mroz, M. (2004). Interactive whole class teaching in the national literacy and numeracy strategies. *British Educational Research Journal, 30*(3), 395–411.

Specjal, S. (2022). Understanding teacher and student talk for optimising teaching, thinking, and learning [Unpublished doctoral dissertation], University of Melbourne.

Thompson, K., Leintz, P., Nevers, B., & Witkowski, S. (2010). The integrative listening model: An approach to teaching and learning listening. In A. D. Wolvin (Ed.), *Listening and human communication in the 21st century* (pp. 266–286). Wiley.

Taylor, S.E. (1964). What research says to the teaching: Listening. Washington, D.C.: Educational Research Association of the National Education Association.

Tyler, M. D. (2001). Resource consumption as a function of topic knowledge in nonnative and native comprehension. *Language Learning, 51*(2), 257–280.

Upshur, J., Koba, H., Spaan, M., & Strowe, L. (1972). *English Language Institute listening comprehension test.* University of Michigan.

Vandergrift, L., & Goh, C. (2009). *Teaching and learning second language listening: Metacognition in action.* Routledge.

Vygotsky, L. S., & Cole, M. (1978). *Mind in society: Development of higher psychological processes.* Harvard University Press.

Watson, K. W., & Barker, L. L. (1984). Listening behavior: Definition and measurement. *Annals of the International Communication Association, 8*(1), 178–197.

Watson, K. W., Barker, L. L., & Roberts, C. V. (1991) *Watson-Barker listening test-High school version.* Innolect.

West, L. (2011). *Accountable talk in the classroom.* https://prezi.com/yogggvuqm4on/accountable-talk-in-the-classroom

West, L. (2012). www.thelearningexchange.ca/?s=Lucy+West

Wilkinson, A., Stratta, L., & Dudley, P. (1976). *Learning through listening.* MacMillan.

Wills, J. (2012). *The self-efficacy of gifted students with a reading disability: The impact of lived experience.* QUT ePrints. http://eprints.qut.edu.au/64452/1/Janelle_Wills_Thesis.pdf

Wills, J. (2020). *Thinking protocols for learning.* Grift Education.

Zammit, S. A. (1991). *LOTE reading and listening tests.* ACER.

INDEX

Helping educators make the greatest impact

CORWIN HAS ONE MISSION: to enhance education through intentional professional learning.

We build long-term relationships with our authors, educators, clients, and associations who partner with us to develop and continuously improve the best evidence-based practices that establish and support lifelong learning.

The Australian Council for Educational Leaders (ACEL) is a not-for-profit organisation uniquely connected with all in the education community who represent the breadth, depth and diversity of the profession. With a focus on leading and leadership at our core, we contribute to and draw from national and global research, practice and learning opportunities through our local branches, conferences, workshops, ACELearn leadership programs, bookshop, online resources and in-house publications. Access to these leadership-focused opportunities is available for classroom teachers through to system leaders.

Learning Forward is a nonprofit, international membership association of learning educators committed to one vision in K–12 education: Equity and excellence in teaching and learning. To realize that vision, Learning Forward pursues its mission to build the capacity of leaders to establish and sustain highly effective professional learning. Information about membership, services, and products is available from www.learningforward.org.